Insight Into Business Processes

A Guide To Understanding And Designing Business Processes

Kenneth J Sherry

To my wife who spent many hours editing and proof reading this book without any remuneration

Table Of Contents

Introduction

In any business today, it is very important to think business processes and what they signify to the business stakeholders and managers. Companies are, in principle, made up of a set of business processes which are fundamental to the strategy and business model, therefore design and implementation are crucial and the keystone to a successful future. If a company ignores the importance of their business processes, it may face the likelihood of employing too many or too few staff or buying technology that is unsuitable for their business process requirements.

Companies have been until recently, to some extent controlled by computer technology and their technical support. *Computer systems and their support should only be utilised when and where needed.* This statement does not diminish the roll of computer systems or the technical support within a company, but puts it in the right prospective.

It is important for the business world to take back control of the company from technology. One way of achieving this, is by business managers to understand the complete requirements of their business processes. Business managers must be responsible for their business processes and the changes that are necessary to achieve efficient and effective processes. The first step towards this goal is to understand the business process.

1   Defining The Business Process

Processes are a part of our lives and are used in different ways. In the past, many industries solved production problems by developing a process and adding machinery to enhance and make the process more effective, in order to satisfy the needs' of the company and its clients.

A business process begins with the customer's needs and ends with the customer's needs fulfilled. A business process is a collection of interrelated tasks or activities that require an input to create an output of a business requirement.

An organisation, whether it be a private company or a public sector, is a collection of business processes. All business process activity can ultimately be performed by people, even in today's technology driven world. However it is not only necessary but also beneficial that technological assistance is utilised to *compliment* the human aspect.

Business processes can be broken down into primary business processes, which are those that directly involve a customer or client, and supporting processes which are administrative, such as human resources, procurement and facilities management.

Business Process Definition

A process is a continuous action, operation or series of changes taking place in a specific manner. The process is made up of tasks, roles, resources and actions to be taken. It must have an owner, be an activity and be driven by inputs and outputs.

The Company

A company is primarily a set of business processes which can be broken down into four main parts; business concept, business strategy, business model and business process management.

During the past decades, technology has driven the business world and software applications have evolved to provide standard solutions for all business requirements. The business world had to accept what was available and whatever solutions the technical department advised, to run the day to day business.

When business concepts and strategies were developed generally, they had to be modified to meet the available technological solutions of the day. This created businesses which were solely modelled around technology and had no way of fully controlling their own destiny.

Today the customer is king and many companies understand this and are very successful.

Companies do not always look at themselves as customers see them and therefore should evolve to become customer oriented. This may mean the business must reinvent itself with a view of looking at the business from the customer's point of view. Business should not look from the inside to the outside but rather the reverse, from the outside of the company looking in. This would result in the business providing what the customer actually needs.

The needs of the customers and providing for these needs within the business model, should be the goal of business process improvement. To achieve this, companies should review their business concepts, business strategy and business model.

Business concepts

A new or existing business requires a concept of ideas and aims positioning it to achieve the company goals. This concept defines what will be achieved and what the outcomes and results of the business will be.

Business strategy

This is the process of specifying the company's mission, vision and objectives, developing policies and plans.

Business model

The term Business Model, is used for a broad range of informal and formal descriptions to represent core aspects of a business. This includes the purpose, offerings, strategies, infrastructure, organisational structures, trading practices, and operational processes and policies. In the most basic sense, a business model is the method of doing business by which a company can sustain itself and generate revenue. The business model defines how a company will position itself in the value chain.

In principle, the business model is a set of processes that constitute the heart of the business which in turn is governed by the business concepts and strategy. The business model is the container for the business processes. These can be improved, modified or new processes implemented, if they are in the realm of the concepts and strategy of the company.

The following diagram shows the relationship between the business concepts, the business strategy, the business model and the business processes.

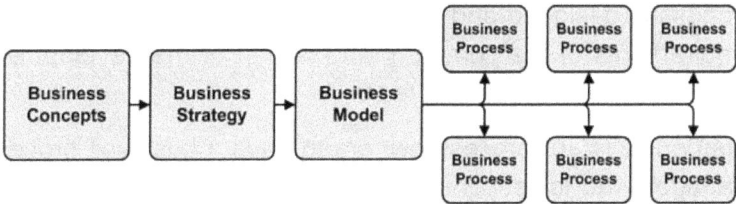

Understanding Business Processes

Do we look at our business through the eyes of our customers? Do we provide the service that we think is required of us? Do customers accept how we do business because they are conditioned to it? Is the customer really king?

In today's society, the customer dictates the business environment. The customer has a choice. The business which provides a service that the customer not only expects, but which exceeds expectations, will keep and expand its customer base.

Continually monitoring the business process and reacting to the customers' interaction with the process will enable the company to understand the customers' needs. There are times when the company must be innovative to produce solutions even though the customer itself is unaware of its needs.

Managing Business Processes

All business processes require a **process owner** who is responsible for the end to end process performance and continuous improvement. The process owner ensures that the process is designed and developed according to the business requirements of the company and is part of the development and implementation review team.

It is beneficial for process owners to have a business process manager who is responsible for the processes. The process manager will use business process analysts, when required, to gather requirements, model and implement the processes.

A Business Process must:

- Have a business process owner
- Have clearly defined boundaries, input and output.
- Have outcomes produced from specified requirements.
- Add value to the existing process
- Be implemented in an organisational structure
- Be clearly documented

Any changes to a business process should be well documented and readily understandable to both the business unit and all those involved in the process.

Business Processes are designed to add value for the customer and should not include unnecessary activities. The outcome of a well designed business process should increase the effectiveness and efficiency for the customer and at less cost to the company.

Summary

- Foremost, a company should consider that efficient and effective business processes will reflect in the profit and loss bottom line.

- Processes are company assets which are designed, controlled and managed within the organisation.

- A company should be flexible and agile, able to react to an ever changing environment.

- Companies should always be ready to review their business processes to listen and react to customer feedback.

NOTES:

2 Introduction To Business Process Modelling

Business process modelling, using graphical models, is the activity of representing the processes of a company. Process modelling is used to capture business activities in a documented form, in order that processes may be analysed and improved.

To describe a business process, a **Business Process Diagram** (BPD) is used which is based on a flowcharting technique, especially for creating graphical models of business processes. Diagrams provide an easy to remember and understandable visualisation of a business process. A BPD is made up of a set of graphical elements and enables the easy development of simple diagrams.

Business process modelling is typically performed by business process analysts and business process managers who are seeking to improve efficiency and quality.

Business process modelling is an activity performed using a modelling tool, to depict both the current state of a company and the desired improved state.

Tasks And Activities

Any activity inside and outside of a company can be classified as a task. A task can be as simple as making breakfast or having a shower. As the day progresses many different tasks which constitute part of a process are completed. Some tasks are repetitive while others are completed only once throughout the process.

Example Of A Daily Process

The process of making dinner for more than one person would follow a process sequence. The following tasks might be necessary before dinner can be served.

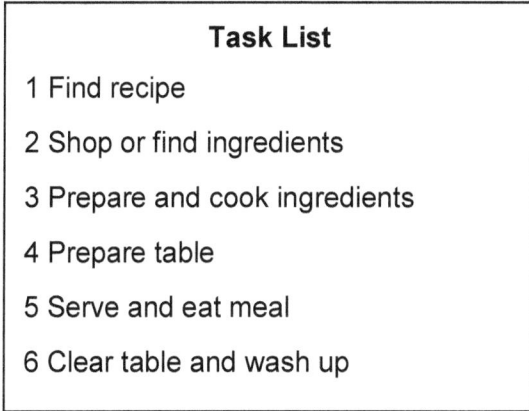

Task List

1 Find recipe

2 Shop or find ingredients

3 Prepare and cook ingredients

4 Prepare table

5 Serve and eat meal

6 Clear table and wash up

The following diagram shows the result of modelling the task list as a sequence flow.

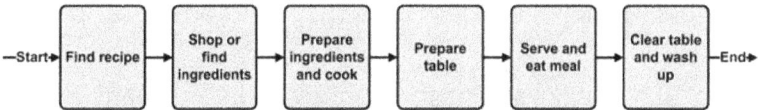

—Start→ Find recipe → Shop or find ingredients → Prepare ingredients and cook → Prepare table → Serve and eat meal → Clear table and wash up —End→

Business Process Modelling Definitions

Business process: is a sequence of tasks, decisions, events and when necessary sub-processes, which contain an aim, an input and an output.

Sub-process: is contained within a complex process and can be composed of groups of tasks, decisions and events which contain an aim, an input and an output.

Task: describes an activity within a process.

Decision: changes the flow of a sequence.

Procedure: is a sequence of actions or instructions to be followed to accomplish a task or solve a problem.

Notation: is a set of graphical symbols for a specific use which replaces a written description.

The Business Process Modelling Notation (BPMN)

In a company environment, it is beneficial to use internationally accepted standards and business process modelling is no exception. Business Process Modelling Notation (BPMN) is supported by the international community and overseen by an organisation, OMG. In the following chapters, BPMN is used to depict the business process model.

Using BPMN allows almost any process to be clearly defined and organised with the minimum of confusion. One of the main reasons that BPMN was developed was to enable the business world to understand diagrammatically what business processes look like. BPMN is set of graphical symbols used to describe a specific business process which can be easily understood by all involved.

Basic Types Of BPMN Elements

Description	Notation
Events are depicted by circles with open centres with internal markers to differentiate between triggers or results. The simplest form of an Event is called a general **START** and **END** event.	◯ ⬤ Start End
A task is represented by a rounded-corner rectangle.	**Task**
A collapsed sub-process notation is a rounded-corner rectangle distinguished by a plus sign in a square at the bottom centre of the shape.	**Collapsed Sub-process** +
The expanded sub-process is shown as a separate diagram with its tasks, sub-processes, decisions and events, required to perform that sub-process. Each expanded sub-process and the corresponding collapsed sub-process should have the same name.	**Expanded sub-process**

Gateways are represented by a diamond shape and are used to control how sequence flows interact as they join and fork within a process.	Gateway
A sequence flow is represented by a solid line with a solid arrowhead and is used to show the order in which tasks or activities are performed in a process.	Sequence flow

Example Of A Daily Process Revisited – Making Dinner

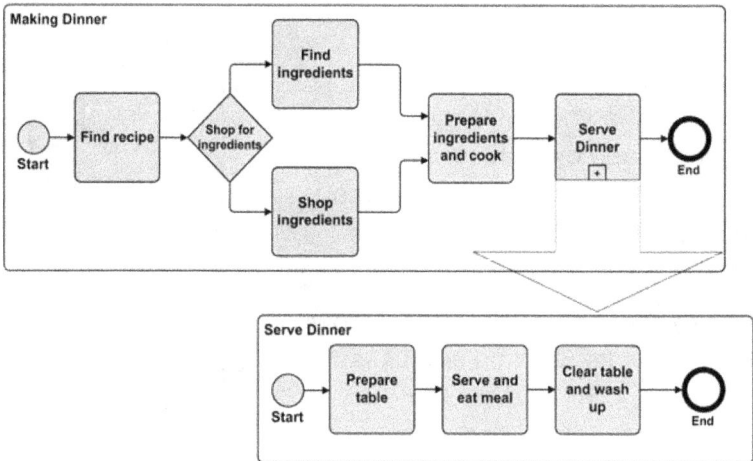

The diagram of making dinner is shown using BPMN elements. The **Start** and **End** events have been introduced. A **Decision** gateway to *Shop for Ingredients* was used to branch the process sequence, to either *Shop for Ingredients* or *Find the Ingredients*.

The sub-process called *Serve Dinner* contains the three tasks, *Prepare table, Serve and eat meal* and the most exciting task of all, *Clear table and wash up*.

The diagram demonstrates the use of a **business process diagram** (BPD) and the techniques used to represent a business process.

Summary

- Any process can be depicted using a modelling notation i.e. Business Process Modelling Notation (BPMN)

- A graphical description of a business process is called a business process diagram (BPD)

- Business Process diagrams must have a start and end event

- Tasks and sub-processes are represented by rectangles and decision gateways by a diamond shape

- The flow from task to task is represented by a sequence flow

3   Basic Business Process Modelling

Modelling a business process requires discovering who, what, when and how tasks are carried out. This may entail talking to people who might have difficulty in explaining what they do. This should not be a stumbling block or deter you. Take their interpretation and create a business process diagram (BPD). When the diagram is completed return to the fulfilment staff (people who carry out the task) for their feedback. This is often a good starting point and involves the fulfilment staff in describing and being part of the process design.

When setting out to model an overall business process, it is recommended to begin with an overall picture of the process, **a high level business process diagram** (BPD) which gives an overall picture. Once the BPD has been designed, then the job of process modelling can begin.

The diagram below illustrates the process of Going to Work which has been broken into two, sequential sub-processes:

1. Getting Ready for Work
2. Commuting to Work.

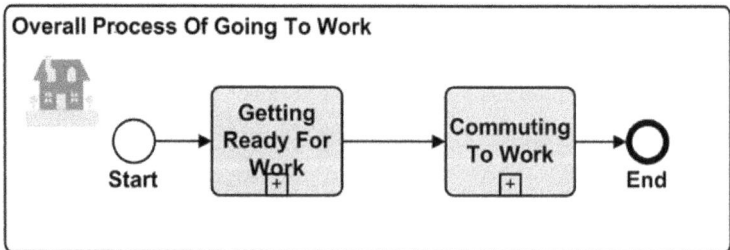

Overall Process Of Going To Work

Start → Getting Ready For Work → Commuting To Work → End

The diagram is a BPD which uses BPMN notations and has a **Start** and an **End** event. As in any process design, all the requirements must be first gathered and then broken down into tasks. These tasks are modelled in a sequential manner to show the flow of each task and where it takes place in the process flow.

Sub-process 1 – Getting Ready For Work

The following is a list of tasks to be performed in Getting Ready for Work which also includes decisions to be made during the process sequence flow.

Getting Ready for Work	
Tasks and decisions involved	**Activity**
Wake up and get out of bed	task
Bathroom or breakfast	decision
Make breakfast	task
Eat breakfast	task
Have a shower	task
Get dressed	task
Dressed and showered	decision
Breakfast	decision
Pick up your bag and keys	task
Close the door and leave	task

Using the task list, the following BPD represents the sub-process of **Getting Ready for Work**.

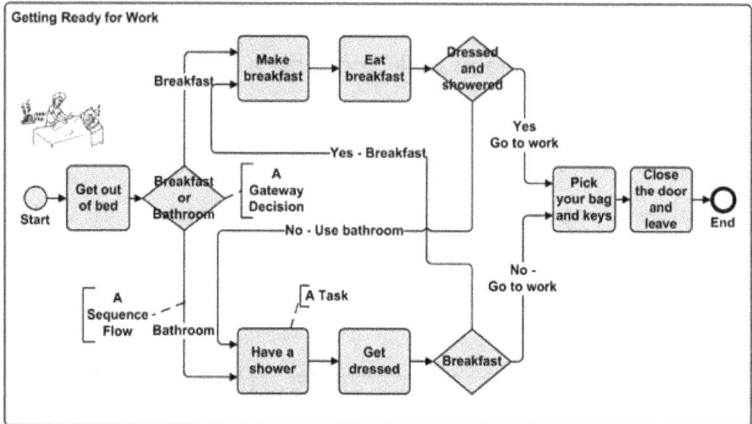

- The above process begins with the **Start** event, activates the **Get out of Bed task**, the sequence then flows to a **Decision** gate (Bathroom or Breakfast)

- Further decisions are made depending on the first decision in the sequence (Bathroom or Breakfast)

- The process sequence flows though more tasks and decisions and finishes with the task **Close the door and leave** and an **End** event

Sub-process 2 - Commuting To Work

The following is a list of tasks to be performed in Commuting to Work which also includes decisions to be made during the process sequence flow.

Commuting to Work task list	
Task and decisions involved	**Activity**
Leave home	task
Take car or bus	decision
Stand and wait for a bus	task
Get on the bus	task
Bus pass or ticket	decision
Buy a ticket find a seat	task
Show pass find a seat	task
Wait for stop	task
Stay on or get off	decision
Walk to exit	task
Press the stop button	task
Bus stops, alight and go to the office	task

Using the task list, the following BPD represents the sub-process **Commuting to Work**

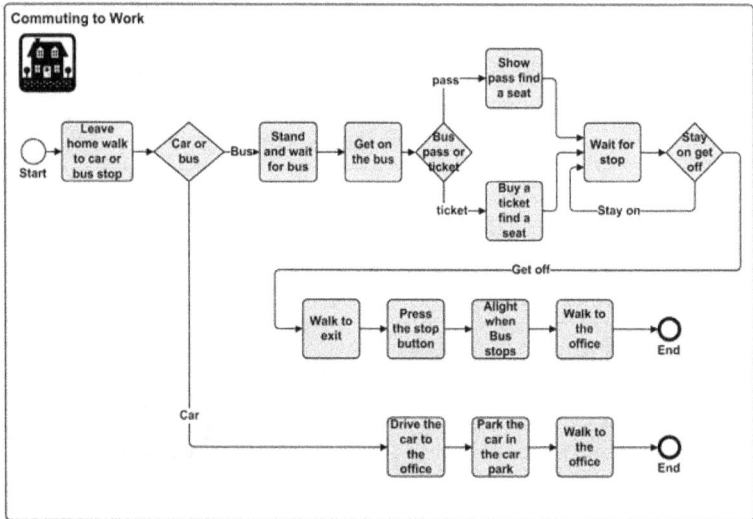

- The Start event activates the leave home task

- If the **decision** is to take the car the sequence goes to Drive the car to the office, Park the car in the car park and Walk to the office, then concludes with an **End** event

- If the **decision** is to take the bus, the sequence flows to further tasks before reaching the **decision,** Bus pass or ticket

- If a ticket must be purchased, the sequence goes to Buy a ticket find a seat task, if not, proceed to Show pass find a seat task

- The process sequence continues until the **decision,** Stay on or get off is reached, then the process task sequence continues through Walk to exit, Press the stop button,

Alight when Bus Stops, Walk to the Office and finally, the **End** event

Task Procedure

A task procedure details the activities within the task and is a sequence of actions or instructions to be followed, to accomplish the task or solve a problem. The procedure of a task will vary, depending on the person, situation, circumstances and timing.

As is shown in BPD **Getting Ready for Work**, each task has a step by step procedure which may be documented depending on the process requirements. The task procedure document could be used by fulfilment staff in a situation which requires a definite procedure to be followed

NOTES:

Example Of A Task Procedure

From the sub-process of Getting Ready for Work the following task procedure describes the task of *Have a shower*. This task procedure outline could be utilised where a step by step procedure is required.

Task procedure for Have a shower	
Procedure number	Procedure step
1	Enter the bathroom
2	Start the shower
3	Adjust to the correct temperature
4	Remove pyjamas
5	Get in the shower
6	Close shower door
7	Find the shower soap
8	Lather up
9	Wash the soap off
10	Turn off shower
11	Get out of the shower
12	Find the towel
13	Towel dry
14	Put on dressing gown
15	Leave the bathroom

Summary

- A process or sub-process is a collection of tasks showing the sequences and creating results

- Each process or sub-process must have a start and an end, an input and output

- The process must have a sequence flow to show how the tasks are joined together, by decisions that are made during the sequence

- A process or sub-process must be an activity and should produce a result

- The business process diagram BPD should be as descriptive as possible, but simple to understand

- It is beneficial to use as much description as possible in the diagram but beware of cluttering up the picture as this deters users from reading the BPD

- Using Business Process Modelling Notation BPMN enables the business analyst to plan and model processes simply, and allows all those involved in the process to read and understand the what and how

4 Modelling Company Business Processes

Company business processes can be complex, however broken down into individual processes they can be defined in such a way, they are easily understood. Many departments are involved in different processes, but the process documentation should only reflect their specific involvement in the selected business process.

It is possible that a business process is specific to only one department but normally, departments are involved in a multitude of different business processes throughout a company. The selected business process, when modelled, should describe the interaction with other parts of the company or other organisations.

The Process Of Acquiring A Workstation

This is a specific business process for requesting a workstation for a new employee. There are two different departments involved

- The department of the new employee

- The IT support department

The departments need to interact between each other to accomplish the process outcome.

Department of the new employee

The following is a business process diagram using BPMN task notations and shows the sequence of tasks when a workstation is requested for a new employee.

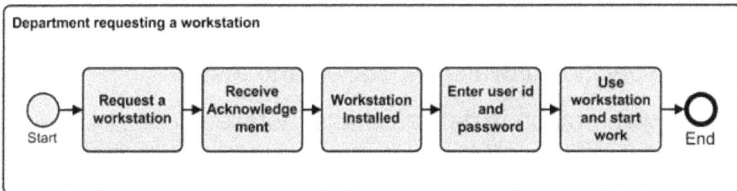

- A request for a workstation for a new employee is sent to the IT department
- The employee receives an acknowledgment that the workstation has been requested
- The workstation is installed
- The employee enters a user id / password
- The employee uses the workstation

IT Support

Below is a business process diagram using BPMN task notations and shows the steps taken by the IT support department when a workstation is requested for a new employee.

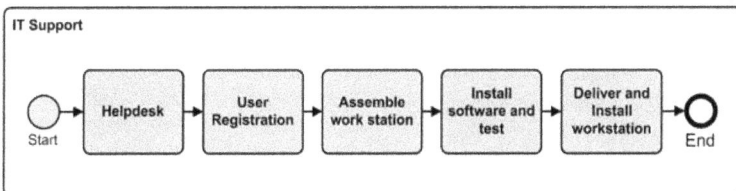

- The IT support helpdesk receives a request for a workstation and the relevant software to be installed for a new employee
- The new employee is registered and informed of the estimated delivery time
- The workstation is assembled and tested
- The specific software is installed and tested
- The workstation is delivered and installed

The Communication Between Two Entities

The **IT support** process runs parallel with the department **requesting a workstation** process. It is necessary to show the communication between the IT support department and the department of the new employee. These are separate departments and therefore do not have a sequence flow connecting them, rather a message flow.

The department **requesting a workstation** is not part of the **IT support** department therefore any communication between them takes the form of messages. This is called a **collaborative process** between the department requesting a workstation and the IT support department. The interaction of the tasks between the two departments is a flow of messages and data objects, such as emails, faxes, letters etc and is called a **message flow**

A **message flow** is used to show the flow of messages between two separate process participants (business entities or business roles) that send and receive the messages. The following is the BPMN message flow notation.

Description	Notation
A message flow is represented by a dashed line with an open arrowhead.	o— — ·Message flow· — ▷

Example Of Communication Between Two Entities

The following is a business process diagram (BPD) depicted using BPMN tasks and describes the communication between the **department requesting a new workstation** with the **IT support**.

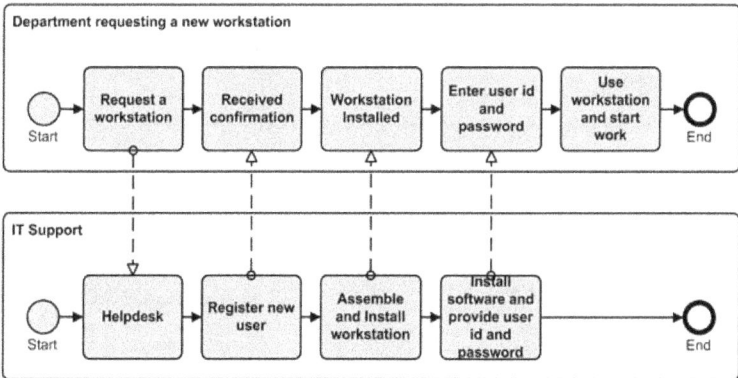

- The request for a workstation is sent to the helpdesk as a message flow, which might be in the form of an email, an internal mail or a phone call, depending on how the organisation is set up

- The help desk registers the new user and responds with a user acknowledgement, providing confirmation that the request has been processed and the employee will receive a workstation
- The IT support assembles and tests the workstation
- The software is installed, configured and tested
- A user id and password is provided

Summary

- When a business process is documented it must only reflect the specific business process
- A business process, when modelled, should describe the interaction between other parts of the company or other organisations
- The communication between the two departments must be through a message flow and is called a collaborative process
- BPMN is designed to cover many types of modelling and allows the creation of sub-processes, as well as end-to-end business processes, at different levels of complexity
- Different entities i.e. different departments, companies or organisations communicate through a message flow, not a sequence flow

5 Process Pools And Swimlanes

Pools allow the process modeller to focus on a single business organisation and are considered **self-contained processes**.

- A **pool** represents a single business organisation e.g. company, department or group
- **Pools** are normally used if the diagram involves two or more separate business entities
- **Pools** are graphical containers used to partition a set of activities
- The sequence flow of the process is contained within the **pool** and cannot cross the boundaries of the **pool**

BPMN Pool	
Description	**Notation**
The **pool** notation is shown as a rectangle either vertical or horizontal	Department or organisation **Pool**

Swimlanes allow the business process modeller to organise and categorise activities of departments or organisations within a pool.

- **Swimlanes** separate the activities of different entities within the process sequence, in order to show the different functional capabilities or responsibilities

- **Swimlanes** are sub-partitions within a **pool** and extend the entire length of the **pool**, either vertically or horizontally

BPMN Swimlanes	
Description	**Notation**
Swimlanes are rectangles within a pool sub-partitioning specific tasks and activities and extend the entire length of the pool.	Department or organisation **Pool** — Department / Department

A Pool With Multiple Swimlanes

The **IT support** process used in the previous chapter has distinct entities, which in the following example have been broken into three different groups and are represented by swimlanes

- IT Service Desk receives the request and registers the user

- Hardware support assembles and tests the workstation

- Software Support installs and tests the software

When the IT Support has a requirement for a new workstation all groups within the department become involved in some part of the process sequence.

- Each group is shown in its own **swimlane**

- Each group works in sequence and in parallel with each other

- The groups are shown in the same **pool** with different sets of tasks

- The individual groups have tasks that do not affect the other groups

The following is a BPD using a **pool** and three **swimlanes** describing the business process of IT Support from receipt of the request to delivery and installation of a new workstation.

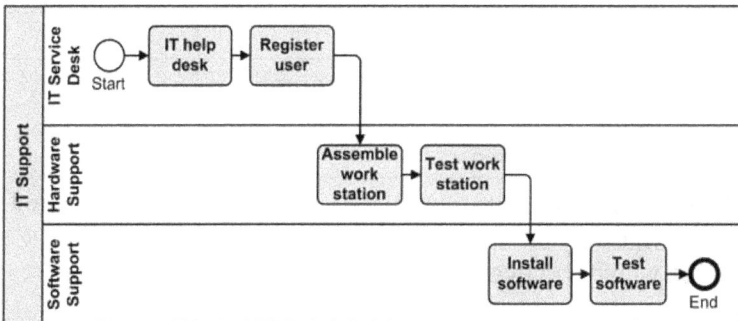

Message Sequence Flow

In the example, **the process of acquiring a workstation** used in the previous chapter, the department of the new employee interacts during the sequence flow, with different groups within the **IT support** department.

Both the **department of the new employee** and the **IT support** are shown in two separate pools, which can only interact using a **message sequence flow**.

Note that the individual pools have a **process sequence flow**.

Message Events

In a previous example a message was used to communicate between the **department of the new employee** and the **IT support**. A further extension of the message flow is the use of **message events**. These events allow the modeller to describe when a message should occur and what the message is used for.

The following table describes the type of **message events** that can be used for communicating with other entities.

BPMN message flow event elements	
Description	**Notation**
Message start events are represented by an envelope inside a single thin circle within the event shape	
Message intermediate events are represented by an envelope inside two thin circles within the event shape. Message intermediate catching events are represented by a non filled envelope. Message intermediate throwing events are represented by a filled envelope.	Catching Event Throwing Event
Message end events are represented by a filled envelope inside a thick circle.	

Message start event notations are used to start a sequence on receiving a message.

There are two notations depicting **Message Intermediate Events** which are only used during the sequence flow, to show some form of message has been sent or received.

- **Message intermediate catching event** notations are used to show that the process sequence flow is being prevented from continuing until a message has been received.

- **Message intermediate throwing event** notations are used to show that a message has been sent during the sequence flow but is not prevented from continuing.

Message end event notations are used to send a message when the process sequence flow is ended.

NOTES:

Collaborative Process

A **collaborative process** is when two different entities communicate with each other using message flows. The diagram below shows an example of a **collaborative process** between the department requesting a new workstation and IT Support department.

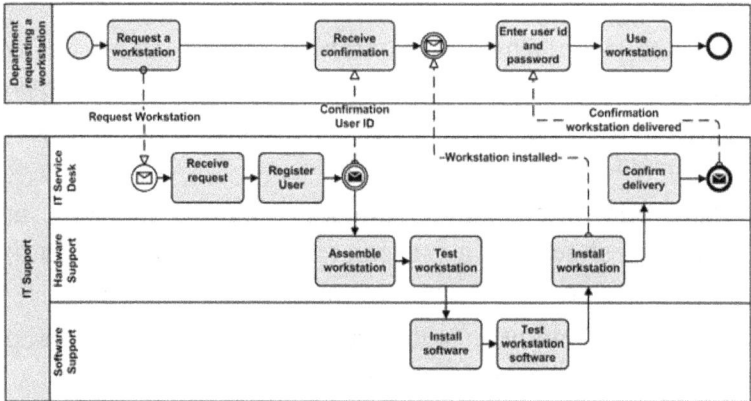

- The overall process is started with a general unspecified **Start Event** from the department requesting a workstation pool

- IT Support pool begins the sequence flow with a **Message Start Event**, and the IT Service Desk (swimlane) receiving a request for a new workstation

- After the user is registered, a message is sent to the department requesting the workstation using a **Message Intermediate Throwing Event**

- A **Message Flow** is sent to the department requesting the workstation, after the workstation is installed

- The department requesting a workstation sequence, waits for the message, the workstation is installed, using a **Message Intermediate Catching Event**

- The department requesting the workstation sequence, ends with a General **End Event**
- The IT Support sequence ends with a **Message End Event**

Summary

- A pool represents a single business organisation e.g. company, department or group
- Swimlanes are sub-partitions within a pool and extend the entire length of the pool, either vertically or horizontally
- A collaboration process depicts the interactions between two or more groups or business entities i.e. pools
- Process sequence flow is confined to a pool and the defined swimlanes and cannot be used to interact with another pool
- Message flows are used to show the interaction of the tasks between process pools
- In this chapter four new notations have been introduced

  Message Start Event

  Message Intermediate Throwing Event

  Message Intermediate catching Event

  Message End Event

6 Black Box And White Box Pools

There are times while modelling processes, when it is not required to know how a process works in another company, department or organisation. In these circumstances, a company or organisation can be represented by a **black box** pool where there are no activities or tasks modelled. In contrast, **white box** pools have tasks and activities which are described in detail.

At some point in a process sequence, there is interaction between a **black box** pool and a **white box** pool using message flows and data objects such as emails, faxes, letters etc.

BPMN Data Object Notation

BPMN **data object** notation (commonly called an artefact) is utilised in a BPD for any type of data that needs to be part of a diagram. The **data object** can also be used as a message description between two process pools.

Data object notation symbolises documents or data which are the results of activities and tasks.

BPMN artefact data object	
Description	**Notation**
Data Object notation is represented by a small rectangle with a folded corner in the top right hand side.	**Data object**

BPMN Association Notation

An **Association notation** is used to link information and artefacts with flow objects. It is used with the **data object** notation.

BPMN artefact association	
Description	Notation
An **Association** is represented by a dotted line with or without an arrowhead.	— -Association— → — -Association— —

NOTES:

BPMN Link Events

The **link intermediate event** notation can be used to make a link, without cluttering the diagram with a long, connecting sequence flow, in an internal BPD. **Link intermediate events** are always used in pairs, **source** intermediate event and **target** intermediate event.

BPMN Link event elements	
Description	**Notation**
The link intermediate **source** event is represented by a black arrow within two thin circles (throwing event)	Throwing
The link intermediate **target** event is represented by a white arrow within two thin circles (catching event)	Catching

The **link intermediate throwing event** is the source of the link and shows the start of the link.

The **link intermediate catching event** is the target of the link and shows the link destination.

The throwing and catching events are a pair as one cannot be used without the other.

Example Of A Collaborative Process

An example of a collaborative process is shown in the following diagram. The information is drawn from the previous chapter showing a **black box** pool replacing, the **requesting a workstation** pool, and introducing a new **black box** pool representing a **Hardware supplier**.

IT support is shown as a **white box** and depicts the tasks and sequence flow of the IT support process.

A Collaborative Process Using Black Boxes

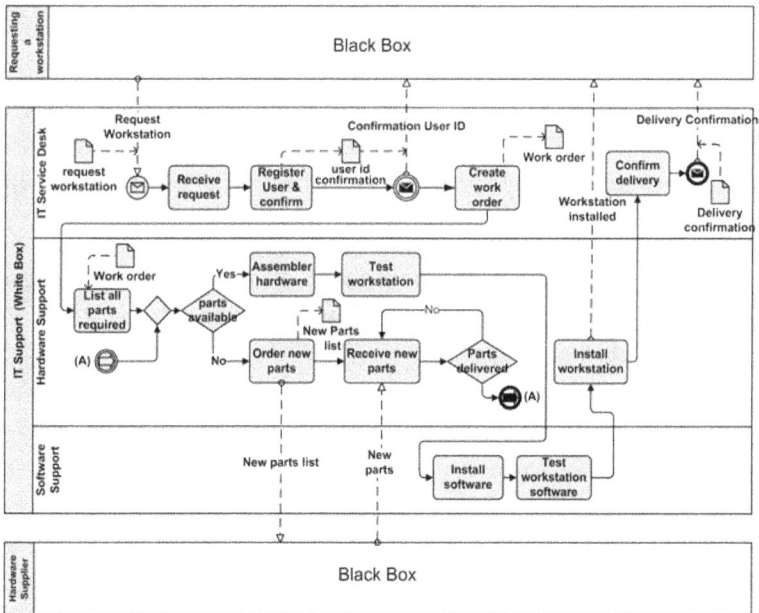

The **IT Support** process sequence begins with a message start event, and the **IT service desk** receiving a request for a workstation, from the **requesting a workstation** process black box pool.

45

The user of the **requesting a workstation** process is registered by the **IT service desk**. A confirmation is created and returned to the **requesting a workstation** black box process pool, through a message flow.

The **IT service desk** creates a work order which is passed to **hardware support**. **Hardware support** checks that all parts are available

If all parts are available the sequence proceeds to assemble the workstation and test workstation tasks.

If parts are unavailable a list of parts to be ordered is documented and shown as a **data object** notation. The parts' list is sent with a message flow to the Hardware supplier, shown as a black box pool.

Hardware support waits until new parts are delivered by the hardware supplier. When the hardware supplier delivers the parts, as shown by a message flow, **Hardware support** continues assembling the workstation and testing.

When the workstation is assembled and tested, the process sequence continues to the **Software support** for software installation and testing.

The **Hardware support** process sequence continues with the installation of the workstation and informs the **requesting a workstation** black box process pool.

IT service desk prepares and sends a confirmation shown as a data object to the user of the **requesting a workstation** process, in the form of a message and the **IT support** process finishes with an end message event.

In the BPD, a **link intermediate event** pair is depicted to prevent cluttering the diagram. The **link intermediate event** pair make the connection from (A) **parts have arrived** (source event) to (A) **all parts available** (target event).

Summary

- Black box process pools do not show any tasks or activities

- White box process pools show all the process tasks and activities in detail, including the related swimlanes

- Message flows can only be used to interact between pools

- The interaction of the tasks between the two process pools is a flow of messages and data objects, such as emails, faxes letters etc.

- Sequence flows can only be used internally within a process pool

- A collaboration process diagram shows the interactions between groups or business entities. These interactions are defined as a sequence of activities, that represent the message exchange patterns between the groups or business entities involved

- Data Objects symbolise documents or data, which are the results of activities and tasks

- The link intermediate event notation can be used to make a process sequence without cluttering the diagram

- Link intermediate events are always used in pairs, source and target

7 Business Process Granularity

Business process **granularity** is used to show the details of a complex business process graphically, in a clear and precise manner.

Showing the details of a business process graphically at different levels is called **decomposing** the business process diagram.

The overall business process design is defined as a **high level** business process diagram. Usually a **high level** business process diagram is sub-divided into specific sub-processes, which are depicted in multiple **medium level** business process diagrams (BPD). The sub-process BPD's can be further decomposed into **low level** BPD's, which show further details of the overall business process.

Low level BPD diagrams can be further decomposed. However too many sub-processes make the overall business process documentation complicated and unmanageable, therefore not user friendly.

The overall diagram is easier to understand by using business process through **granularity**. The question should be asked how far should the diagrams be **decomposed?** A basic test is to document the task procedures and if they appear complicated, then it might be logical to make them a sub-process.

Granularity Diagram

The granularity diagram below is an example of how business process documentation is decomposed, using **high level**, **medium level** and **low level** BPD.

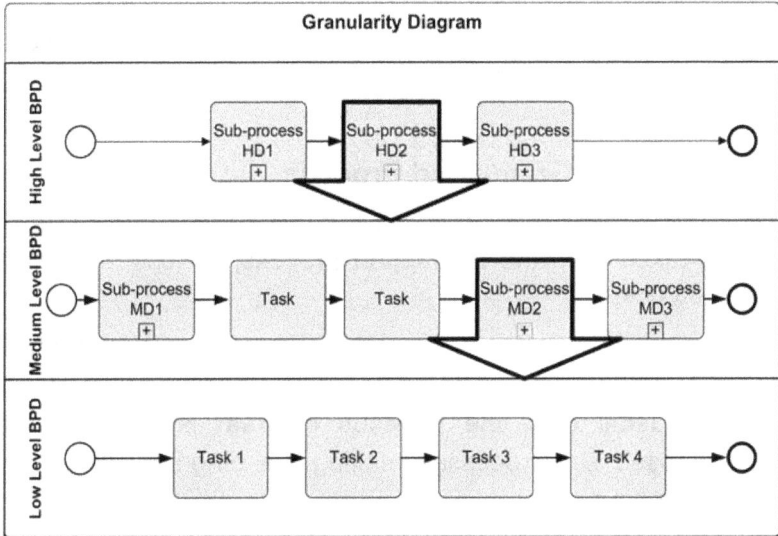

High Level BPD

In general, a high level BPD shows the overall business process. Each high level process is a series of collapsed sub-process.

Medium Level BPD

A medium level BPD is an expanded sub-process of one of the high level collapsed sub-processes. In this example Sub-process HD2 which is a sequence of collapsed sub-processes and tasks.

Low Level BPD

A low level BPD is an expanded sub-process from a medium level BPD. In this instance Sub-process MD2 is a sequence of tasks and decisions.

It is possible to include a collapsed sub-process in a low level BPD creating a forth level of complexity. Further sub levels can be modelled at the analyst's discretion.

Example Of A Granulated Process

The following diagram is an example of granulated BPD's and is taken from the IT Support process, described in a previous chapter.

- The overall business process, **IT Support,** is a high level BPD showing the pools and swimlanes of the department. The detail from the previous diagram is replaced by collapsed sub-processes making the diagram simpler to understand

- The sub-process, **assemble workstation and test**, is expanded into a separate medium level BPD

- The sub-process, **test workstation,** is expanded into a low level BPD

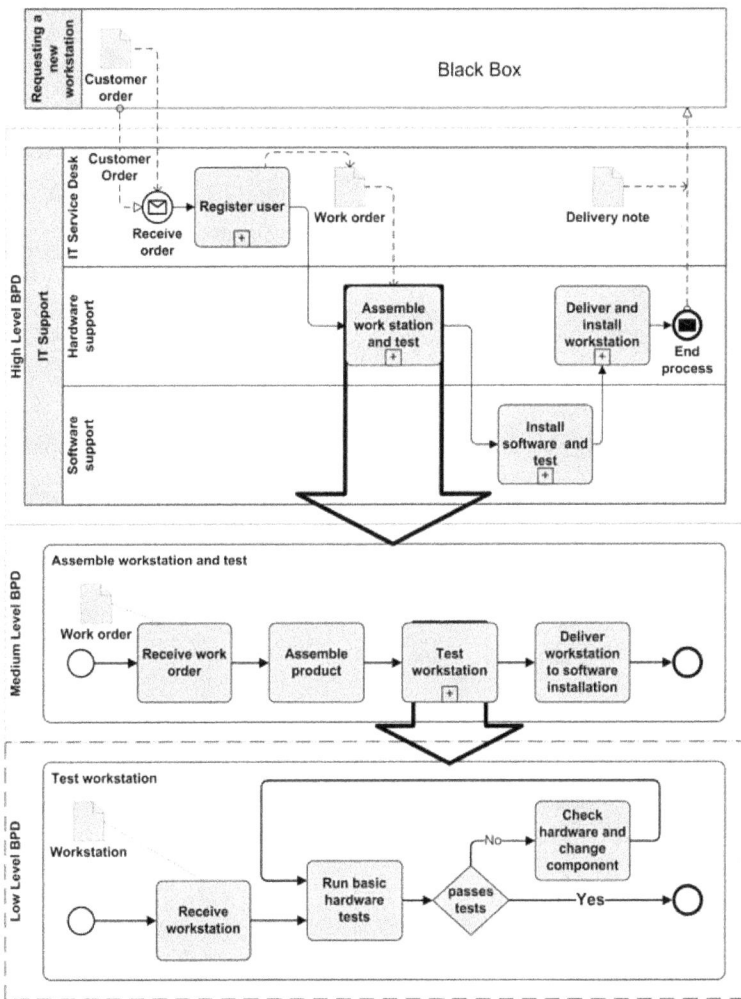

Requesting a new workstation (High Level BPD)

Customer order — Black Box

IT Service Desk

Customer Order → Receive order → Register user → Work order — Delivery note

Hardware support

Assemble work station and test → Deliver and install workstation → End process

Software support

Install software and test

Medium Level BPD

Assemble workstation and test

Work order → ○ → Receive work order → Assemble product → Test workstation → Deliver workstation to software installation → ○

Low Level BPD

Test workstation

Workstation

○ → Receive workstation → Run basic hardware tests → passes tests — No → Check hardware and change component

passes tests — Yes → ○

51

Summary

- Business process **granularity** is used to show the details of a complex business process graphically
- Detailing the overall business process into sub-processes is called **decomposing** the BPD
- There are three main levels of granularity

    High level BPD

    Medium level BPD

    Low level BPD

- Further levels of decomposition can be considered but the question must be asked; is it a task, a procedure for doing something or a sub-process?
- Instead of making multiple levels of granularity it may be better to have more sub-processes in the **high level** BPD

NOTES:

8 Business Rules

If everyone within an organisation understands what they are doing, why they are doing it and when they should be doing it, logically the operation would be more efficient and therefore more effective.

Before designing or modelling any business process it is necessary to determine how the organisation does business. This can only happen using rules which are comprehensible to all those involved. These are called **business rules**. Business rules specify how and when tasks within a business process are fulfilled.

Business Rule Definition

A **business rule** is a statement that defines what, how and when some aspects of the business are fulfilled. A **business rule** is intended to assert business structure, to control, or influence the behaviour of the company.

From a business perspective, a **business rule** pertains to what, how and when it is applied to the behaviour of people in a company, from working hours, restrictions on smoking to procedures for filling out a purchase order.

From an information system perspective, a **business rule** pertains to the facts which are recorded as data and controls the changes to the values of those facts. A **business rule** denotes specific constraints on the creation, updating, and removal of data in an information system.

Typical Business Rules That Affect Employees

Every company has rules that affect the way the company operates and what is expected from its employees. Many business rules are not apparent and are normally accepted without the realisation that they are, in fact, a business rule. Here are a few examples;

- No smoking is a business rule and defines that smoking is not allowed in a specific areas.

- Unauthorised cars will be towed away.

- The parking area has a speed limit of 10 miles per hour

- No food or drinks permitted at the work place

- Clean desk policy after working hours

There are many such rules which are part of the employee's way of life and normally accepted as a matter of course but constitute the way a company operates.

The following are examples of **contractual business rules** for employees

- Start work at 9:00

- Block hours for working 9:00 through 11:00 and 13:00 through 16:00

- Dress code Monday through Thursday is business dress, on Fridays informal

- Mid-morning break is between 10:15 and 10:45 for 15 minutes

- Lunch is between 12:00 and 13:30 for 45 minutes, which is deducted from the working day

- Afternoon break is between 15:00 and 15:30 for 15 minutes

- Working not permitted after 19:00, unless with special permission as security closes the building

Company Business Rules

Business rules affect how a company deals with clients, customers and vendors alike. There are many business rules that can be applied depending on the type and size of company. Large international companies may even have different rules depending on the country.

Business rules not only affect clients and customers but also suppliers of services to that company. The service a company provides may be influenced by their vendors. This can have a knock on effect involving the vendors and their suppliers.

The service that the company provides to their clients is defined in a **Service Level Agreement** (SLA). Web services define their services under Terms and Conditions (T&C). A company will also have an agreement with its suppliers.

A Company Service Level Agreement

Business rules are fundamental to any business process and are used to provide a Service Level Agreement (SLA), which defines what type of service the company provides to its customers.

The SLA is a contract between a company and its customers or clients. How the rules are defined in a SLA is crucial to the business outcome.

Company Service Agreement Relationship

The following diagram shows the service relationship between the company and its suppliers and the company and its customers or clients.

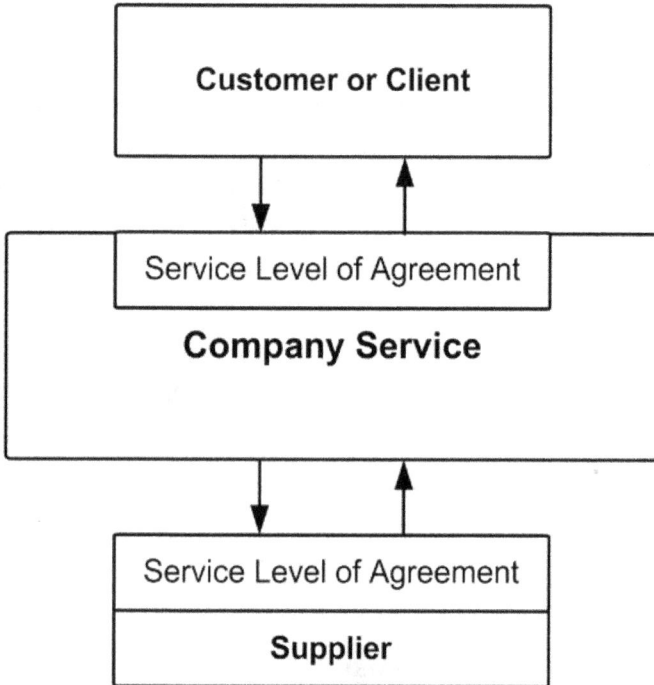

```
┌─────────────────────────────────────┐
│                                     │
│        Customer or Client           │
│                                     │
└─────────────────────────────────────┘
        │           ▲
        ▼           │
┌─────────────────────────────────────┐
│  ┌──────────────────────────────┐   │
│  │  Service Level of Agreement  │   │
│  └──────────────────────────────┘   │
│         Company Service             │
│                                     │
└─────────────────────────────────────┘
        │           ▲
        ▼           │
┌─────────────────────────────────────┐
│    Service Level of Agreement       │
├─────────────────────────────────────┤
│            Supplier                 │
└─────────────────────────────────────┘
```

Basis Of A Service Level Agreement

Here are some general business rules which could be included in a SLA.

Normal working hours: The hours that a client can expect the company to supply services during a normal working day.

Out of hours service: The hours that a client can expect a business to supply services out of normal working hours.

Company responses: The time a client can expect a company to respond to a request within a working day and out of hours.

Product deliveries: The time scale in which products can be expected to be delivered.

Credit reference: A company demands specific requirements about clients before a product is delivered.

Invoice payments: Invoices must be paid within a fixed period.

Emails to clients and vendors: Email response time is the maximum time that a client or vendor can expect an email in response to an email request.

Telephone to clients and vendors: If the company telephone is not answered within a specific time period, the caller will be transferred to an automatic answer system.

Signature on company documents: Company requires one or more signatures depending on the type of document.

Official document: A fax or a scanned document in a PDF format sent by email is accepted as an official document.

Company procurement: Company policy defines the limit of expenditure and the number of tenders.

Summary

- There are endless business rules encountered while working for a company

- Some business rules are very useful and define how the company does business, while others seem superfluous

- When modelling processes, it is important to understand the company business rules

- When business rules are changed or improved, It is important the business process documentation is updated

- Business rules affect how a company deals with clients, customers and vendors alike

- A business rule denotes specific constraints on the creation, updating, and removal of data in an information system

- The business process is governed by the business rules and therefore must be part of the process modelling

- Business rules can be considered the guideline framework of a business process

9 Business Process Management

The term **Business Process Management** (BPM) refers to the analysis, design, implementation and optimisation of enterprise-wide business activities, and encompasses strategy, processes, people and technology.

The most effective way to drive BPM is from, outside in (customer first) and top down (company strategy). Management must be involved and committed to this method of doing business, as without this commitment BPM will not provide the expected results. The following are four aspects which are crucial at all stages of business process improvement.

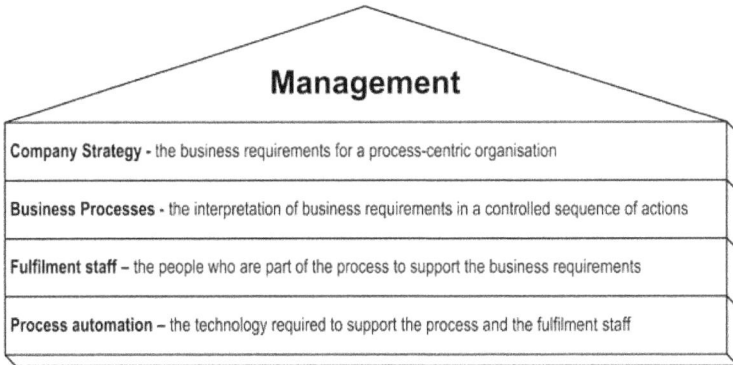

Management

Company Strategy - the business requirements for a process-centric organisation	
Business Processes - the interpretation of business requirements in a controlled sequence of actions	
Fulfilment staff – the people who are part of the process to support the business requirements	
Process automation – the technology required to support the process and the fulfilment staff	

Company Strategy

Historically, one of the greatest deficiencies of previous approaches to business change has been the failure to place the process improvement initiative in a truly strategic context. Strategy is defined throughout an organisation as setting targets and objectives that emphasise the roles and outcomes, balanced against available time, resources and ongoing commitments.

Business Processes

The customer is at the heart of the core concept of business processes and the reason for change. Change and improvement is necessary in any organisation as customer requirements evolve. Processes should be designed to create value for the customer, which in turn affects the bottom line for shareholders.

When a business process improvement is required and there is no up to date documentation, the analyst should determine the current business process situation. The business process improvement documentation takes into account the current situation and the required business process improvements.

Process improvement reviews should always refer to the agreed strategy. Ongoing reference to company strategy helps to ensure the effective use of resources and focus on process outcomes.

Fulfilment Staff

People are a unique resource and have a direct influence on customer outcomes. The success of a company depends on strategy, processes and staff, rather than processes and technology. Staff, with the correct training and understanding of the process, are the business's greatest asset. Fulfilment staff involved in the business process should be kept fully up to date with the changes and the technology used.

It must be understood that any process improvement should be considered carefully due to people's concept of change. If fulfilment staff are part of the process improvement team, they will be more willing to accept any new changes.

The fulfilment staff are normally on the front line of customer outcomes and must sometimes accept and deal with the inadequacies of badly implemented processes. The information accrued by the fulfilment staff is an invaluable input to any process improvement.

Process Automation

Technology is a collection of tools used as part of the process to accomplish customer outcomes. For many years technology has driven the business process, resulting in processes being designed around the available technology.

There is a general awareness of the benefits of using the most up to date technology within business. Is it really necessary? How and where information is handled, is of little importance to the customer. The process first needs to be designed and then the people and technology integrated into the tasks and activities.

The technological requirements should be established after the business process has been documented and approved. This prevents technology being purchased which does not correspond to the process requirements.

Summary

- The external focus is one of the main points in BPM and needs to be supported by management
- If BPM is to be successful, it must include interfacing with all company functions, not just incremental process improvements

10 End To End BPM Improvement Process

The BPM **improvement process** allows management to design and develop improved business processes. Designing improved business processes should be sequential, allowing the design to take a step by step approach, with the ultimate delivery of the improved process emulating the business requirements.

The aim of the improvement process is to ensure the business process design corresponds to the business requirements. This is achieved by regular review meetings referencing the business requirements, as the business process improvement framework.

The Process Of Improving Business Process

End to end business process management is the complete life cycle of a process improvement. The following diagram illustrates the complete process design life cycle.

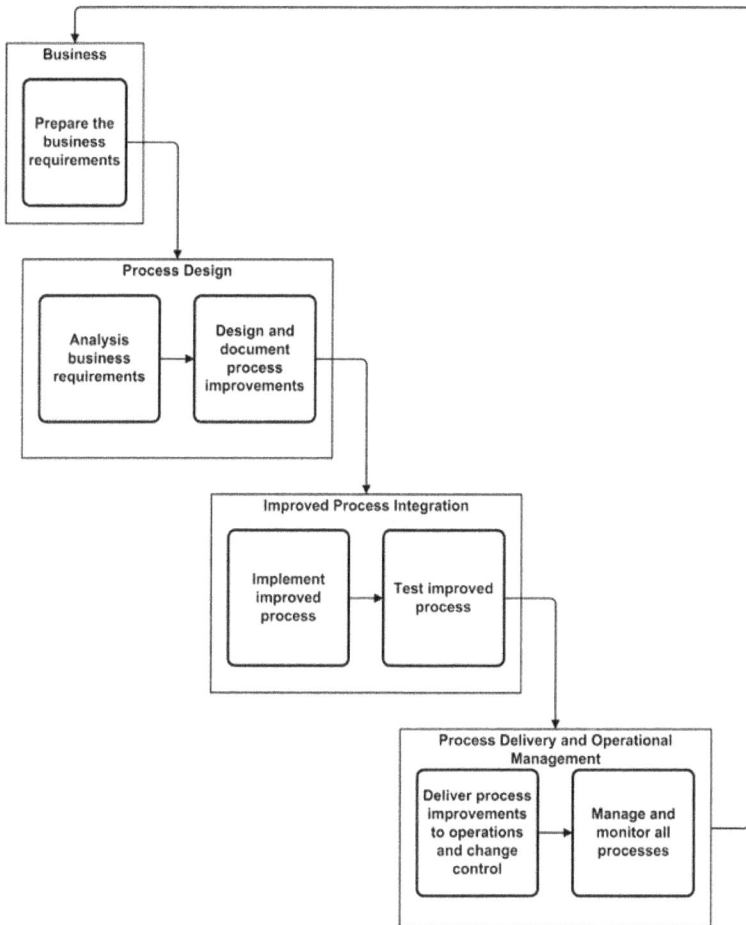

Business

Prepare the business requirements

Process Design

Analysis business requirements

Design and document process improvements

Improved Process Integration

Implement improved process

Test improved process

Process Delivery and Operational Management

Deliver process improvements to operations and change control

Manage and monitor all processes

Description Of The Improvement Business Process

Business

When a business process improvement is requested, the management should detail the **business requirements** reflected by the business strategy and document the necessary business process improvements.

Process design

After the **business requirements** are analysed, the improved process is designed and documented accordingly. If a current process is already documented, then it should be updated with the new design improvement.

Improved process Integration

Fulfilment staff are designated and technology is implemented for a new process. Staff should be evaluated to establish if training is required. The technology should be assessed for the process design suitability. The complete process, including the improved process, is tested to determine whether staff and technology produce the required outcomes.

Change management must be involved to determine changes in technology and the impact of any future changes that might take place.

Process delivery and operational management

Once the process is in place it is handed over to operations. The improved process is monitored regularly along with any other processes which may be affected.

It is important that change management and process control take ownership of the process documentation. Operations should monitor all processes and report any discrepancies that occur.

Summary

- The improved process must reflect the business strategy and the defined business requirements

- The improved process must meet the needs and requirements of the customer

- Allocate staff for specific tasks and ensure training is provided

- Some business processes can be improved without new technology being introduced

- Technology must accommodate the process requirements for the fulfilment staff to produce the correct outcomes

NOTES:

11 Gathering Business Process Requirements

Any new or improved business process needs the requirements gathered, analysed and documented. Once the initial requirements are documented, more detailed documents can be developed, depending on the requirements.

Although business processes differ from company to company, the principles are the same.

Requirements Gathering

Gathering requirements can be a long and arduous process during which many delicate psychological skills are involved. New system environment or new ways of working and relationships between people can cause anxiety amongst employees. It is important to identify all the stakeholders, take into account their needs and ensure the implications of the new process are understood.

There are three different sequential activities used to gather and document the business process requirements.

Elicit Requirements

This is the task of communicating with business managers and fulfilment staff to determine and gather requirements. Analysts can employ several techniques which may include personal or team interviews and requirements workshops.

Analyse Gathered Requirements

Analyse and determine whether the stated requirements are clear, complete, ambiguous or contradictory. It may be necessary to repeat interviews and workshop to obtain more accurate information. Ensure the information is as complete as possible before recording the requirements.

Record Requirements

The requirements can be documented in various forms, such as natural-language documents, requirements' list or pure process specifications. It is important that the documentation is user friendly and can be understood by the business, stakeholders and staff alike. If the documentation does not reflect the actual requirements, the process improvement will fail. The documents should at least be company standard or a recommended industrial standard. It is vital that all process documentation follows the same standard in all aspects.

Good and accurate requirements documentation is paramount to any business process improvement and should not be underestimated.

Gathering And Documenting Business Process Requirements

Below is a diagram depicting the process of gathering and documenting business process requirements.

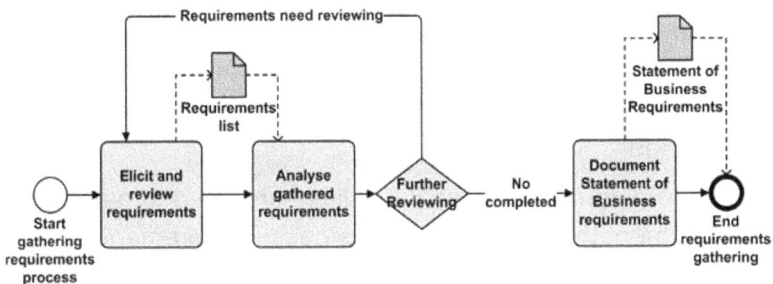

Gathering requirements process sequence

- Start by eliciting the requirements from those involved in the new business process
- List all the new business process requirements
- Analyze the list of requirements for ambiguity, duplication and plain language
- Review requirements where and when necessary
- Record requirements in a **statement of business requirements**

The business requirements process needs several review stages before the final document is signed off by the stakeholders and the process owner.

Summary

- The business process owner is the person responsible for the business process should have a business case approved before producing any process requirements documentation
- Stakeholders need to be involved to established their needs
- The process owner should produce a document which outlines the requirements of the new or improved process. This is normally done in conjunction with the process manager
- Three different sequential activities are used to gather and document the Statement of Business Requirements
  - Elicit requirements
  - Analysis gathered requirements
  - Record requirements

- Analysts can employ techniques including
    - Personal interviews
    - Team interviews
    - Requirement workshops
- Ensure the information is as complete as possible before documenting the requirements
- The documents should reflect the actual requirements
- Recorded requirements should be user friendly and be understood by the business and stakeholders

NOTES:

12 Business Process Documentation Overview

This chapter outlines the principle documentation required when developing new or improved business processes. The documents are created in the following sequence

1. Statement of Business Requirements
2. Business Process Map
3. Fulfilment Tasks

After each document is produced, a review should take place with process owner, process manager and stakeholders. This review should clarify that the documentation reflects the business requirements.

Statement Of Business Requirements

The first step in documenting a new or improved business process is to create a **statement of business requirements**. The **statement of business requirements** describes how a business process is to be performed for a new or improved business process and should include an overview of the new or improved business process and the reasons for any changes.

This document can be used as part of the acceptance procedure and a measurement of completion, while the business process is being developed.

The **statement of business requirements** is prepared by the process owner in conjunction the process manager. This document should be in a form that can be used and understood by all parties concerned in the new or improved business process.

Business Process Map

The business process analyst develops a **business process map** upon completion of the **statement of business requirements** comprising of the following.

Business process description

The overall business process description describes how the process is achieved including all the relevant detail.

Business process overview

This is a high level business process diagram outlining the sub-process and the sequence flow.

Business process document flow

This describes the documents that are produced for the customer and internal documents, which are required for the process.

Business process sequence flow

This describes the process sequence flow, the documents needed and the input and output documents required.

Sub- process descriptions

Each sub-process has separate documents which include.

- Sub-process description
- Sub-process model

Fulfilment Task Documents

Fulfilment task procedure

A **fulfilment task procedure** document is a description of the steps which are to be followed by the person or persons carrying out the task. This document is used by business process fulfilment staff as a guideline to carrying out the procedure.

Task method statement

A **task method statement** is a document that details the way a process task is to be completed and includes.

- an outline of any hazards involved
- a step by step guide on how to do the task safely
- details of the control measures that are introduced, to ensure the safety of everyone who is affected by the task

The business process manager should outline what is required for each process task, in conjunction with the process owner. This should take into account the sequence of steps needed to complete a process task safely, with the minimum risk possible to the person or persons carrying out the task.

Task method statement is a working level document that provides a description of the work to be undertaken. The **task method statement** should highlight any significant hazards, as well as hazards that could result from an associated task.

Summary

- It is important to set out the document requirements before developing any new business processes or improving existing processes

- Start with a **statement of business requirements** document which is to be completed by the business process owner

- A **statement of business requirements** document describes how a business process is to be performed

- Upon completion of the **statement of business requirements** document, the process manager and the process analyst in conjunction with the process owner, create a **business process description** document

- A **business process map** describes how the process will be achieved and includes all the relevant detail

- A **task method statement** is a sequence of steps to be adhered to, to reduce any risks including all health and safety aspects such as personal protective equipment requirements etc

- A **task procedure** is a series of steps which are written down and followed by the person carrying out the task

13   Statement Of Business Requirements

The **statement of business requirements** is a comprehensive document outlining the requirements of a new or improved business process. It is very important that the document is complete and reflects the business requirements, before delivery to the process manager or analyst. The **statement of business requirements** is produced by a requirements gathering team which includes

- Stakeholders
- Process owner
- Process manager
- Process analyst
- Selected fulfilment staff

Document Overview

The following is a guideline for a **statement of business requirements** document.

Company
> Company name

Business process name
> The name of the process

Business process owner
> The name and position of the process owner

Business process manager
> The name and position of the process manager

Business process overview

This is a narrative view of the overall requirements of a new or improved process

Business process method

This describes how the process will be performed

Resources

This describes the resources associated with the delivery of the process, largely drawn from the service requirements of other processes, internal or external.

Business rules

The required business rules are described and documented.

Regulations

Regulations that influence the process are described and documented, such as internal and external company standards.

Dependencies

Process dependences, which influence the process activities, are described, including the use of appropriate standard tools.

Implementation plans

This is a statement of the business process owner's plans for the new or improved business process use and implementation.

Example Of A Statement Of Business Requirements

The following example shows how a **statement of business requirements** is used to outline the requirements of a new business process.

In this example, a Computer Hardware Supplier company documents a new process allowing customers to purchase products to order.

The business process is called, Computer Products to Customer Order.

The **statement of business requirements** document describes how the new business process Computer Products to Customer Order, is to be accomplished.

This example of a statement of business requirements document is only a guideline and does not reflect any actual business process or company.

The Statement Of Business Requirements

Company

Computer Hardware Supplier

Business process name

Computer Products to Customer Order

Business process owner

To be designated

Business process manager

To be designated

Business process overview

The company will produce computer products to customer order delivery within 15 working days. The customer is informed at all stages of the process i.e. confirmation of order, confirmation of delivery, delivery note and an invoice if applicable. Product parts will be either on stock or ordered from a parts manufacture. After the products are assembled and tested, they are packed and delivered to the customer.

Business process method

The process starts with an order from a customer which is handled by the back office department. The back office department checks the customer credit rating and confirms acceptance of the order.

The customer order is reviewed by the back office and a work order created detailing the specific customer requirements.

The work order is checked for parts on stock and a confirmation of delivery is produced, informing the customer of the delivery schedule. The work order proceeds to product assembly and test department, where the required product is produced.

Once the product is ready an invoice and a delivery note are prepared. The product is packed and shipped by an outsourced company.

Resources

The finance department is required to respond and to advise on customer credit checks.

Business rules

The company will supply a fully tested computer within 15 working days from order.

The order details must reflect the customer's exact requirements.

An order confirmation is sent to the customer specifying the original requirements, the cost of the products(s) and the terms of payment.

The customer has two workings days to respond to any order conflicts.

A confirmation is sent to the customer within two working days stating the delivery schedule.

Invoices are paid within 30 days from delivery or COD.

Regulations

The products are tested to meet the statutory electrical safety standards.

Dependencies

The process is dependent on any ordered parts being delivered on time from the parts supplier.

Delivery of the products depends on the products being shipped on time, by an outsourced company, to the customer.

Implementation plans

It is expected that the business process design will take 60 days to complete and implementation and testing will be a further 30 days

Summary

- It is important that the business process owner reviews all the requirements and confirms the accuracy, before delivery to the process manager or business process analyst.

- The process manager and business process analyst are part of the team gathering the requirements, however the decisions are made by the business owner.

- The business owner should have full responsibility for the requirements gathering process

NOTES:

14 Documenting A Business Process Map

Before starting to develop a new business process or improve an existing business process it is necessary to create the required documentation.

The **business process map** is developed upon completion of the Statement of Business Requirements and contains the following.

1) Business process description

2) Business process overview

3) Business document flow

4) Business process sequence

These documents are produced by the business process analyst in conjunction with the business process owner and stakeholders. The documents must be comprehensive and understandable to all parties before proceeding further. It is very important that the documentation is complete and reflects the business requirements.

To show the use of these documents the **statement of business requirements**, from the previous chapter, is used as an example. These documents describe how the business process, **computer products to customer order**, is to be executed within the framework of the business requirements.

Collating A Business Process Map

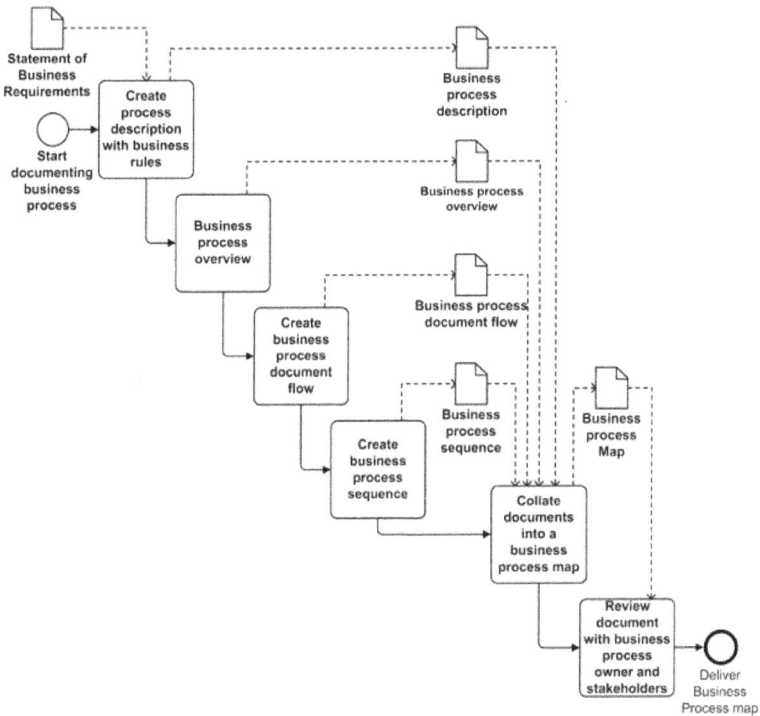

Business Process Description

The business process analyst is responsible for developing the **business process description**, taking the information from the statement of business requirements. The **business process description** describes how the process is achieved including all the relevant detail.

Business Process Description Document Example

Business process name

Computer products to customer order

Business process owner

To be designated

Business process analyst

To be designated

Sub-processes

1. Receive and process order
2. Assemble components and test
3. Create invoice and delivery note
4. Pack and ship product

Process description

The business process starts when an order is received for new computer products. The customer is sent an order confirmation. The parts availability is checked and parts ordered from a parts supplier, if necessary. When all parts are available, the computer is assembled and tested before the specific software is installed. The products are delivered by an outsourced company.

Process trigger

The process is triggered by a customer order for computer products.

Process results

The computer or computers will be assembled, tested and delivered to the customer with an invoice to be paid with 30 days or COD.

Process inputs

- Customer detailed email
- Customer fax

Process outputs

- Delivery schedule
- Computer products
- Delivery note
- Invoice

Process business rules

- The hardware will be delivered within 15 working days from order
- Customer receives an order confirmation within one working day
- Customer receives a product delivery schedule within three working days from order
- Customer is informed of any delays to the delivery schedule within two working days
- Invoice is sent, if the customer is credit worthy, when product is ready to be shipped
- Invoice is included with the product and delivery note for COD payment if the customer is not credit worthy
- Outsource shipping company will have three days to deliver products

Process interfaces

- Customer
- Parts supplier
- Outsourced shipping company
- Finance department

Process notes

The process design is only concerned with the process sequence of the Hardware Supplier Co. and not with any other entity, although there are interface requirements to other companies.

The finance department is required to respond and to advise on customer credit worthiness.

Business Process Overview

Upon completion of the **business process description** the process analyst proceeds to produces a **business process overview** outlining the sub-process and the process timing. The **business process overview** shows collapsed sub-processes requiring a BPD to describe each sub-process.

Business Process Overview Document Example

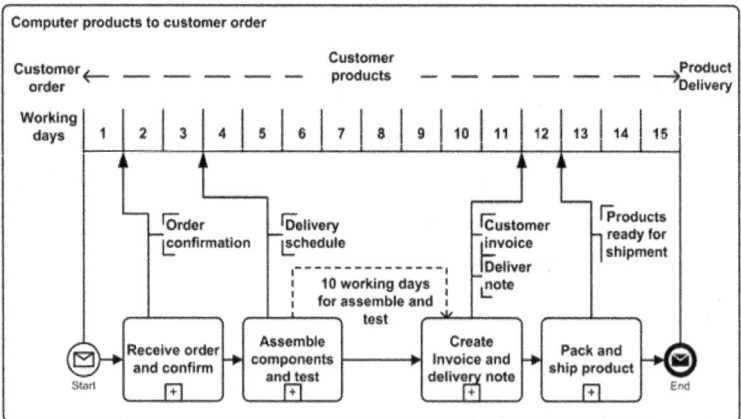

Business process overview description

The **computer products to customer order** process requires four sub-processes to complete the business process. Each sub-process follows in sequence, as one must be completed before the next starts. There is one input, the **customer order**, which is received by email or fax. The total time from order to product received by the customer, is a maximum of 15 working days.

Business process overview process timing

- The process timing shows that the products are ready for shipment three working days before the customer receives the products, to allow the shipping company time to deliver.

- The customer invoice and the delivery note are completed one day after receiving the completed **work order**.

- The **assemble components and test** sub-process has a maximum of 10 working days to provide fully tested products. The timing will also depend on receiving the ordered components from the parts supplier.

- The delivery schedule is sent three days after receiving the customer requirements from receive order and confirm sub-process. The delivery schedule will depend on the estimated date of delivery from the parts supplier.

- The receive order and confirm sub-process has one working day to check the order and send the confirmation to the customer, after receiving the customer order. During this time, the credit worthiness of the customer must be checked and the customer requirements document must be completed.

Business Process Document Flow

The **business process document flow** is produced by the business process analyst. This document describes the process documents that are to be produced for the customer and also the required internal documents.

Business Process Document Flow Example

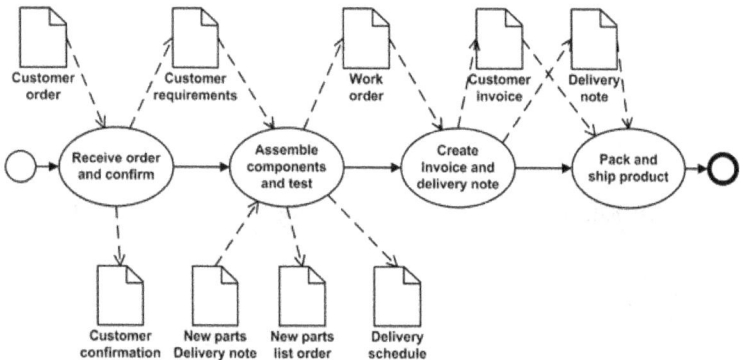

Business process document description

The **computer products to customer order** process produces four documents which are sent to the customer

- Customer order confirmation
- Delivery schedule
- Customer invoice
- Delivery note

Three internal documents

- Customer requirements
- Parts order used to request parts from the parts supplier
- Work order used as an internal document throughout the product assembly and testing

Business Process Sequence

The business process analyst produces a business process sequence outlining the departments involved. The following BPD describes the business process sequence and where and when documents are an input and where documents are produced.

Business Process Sequence Document Example

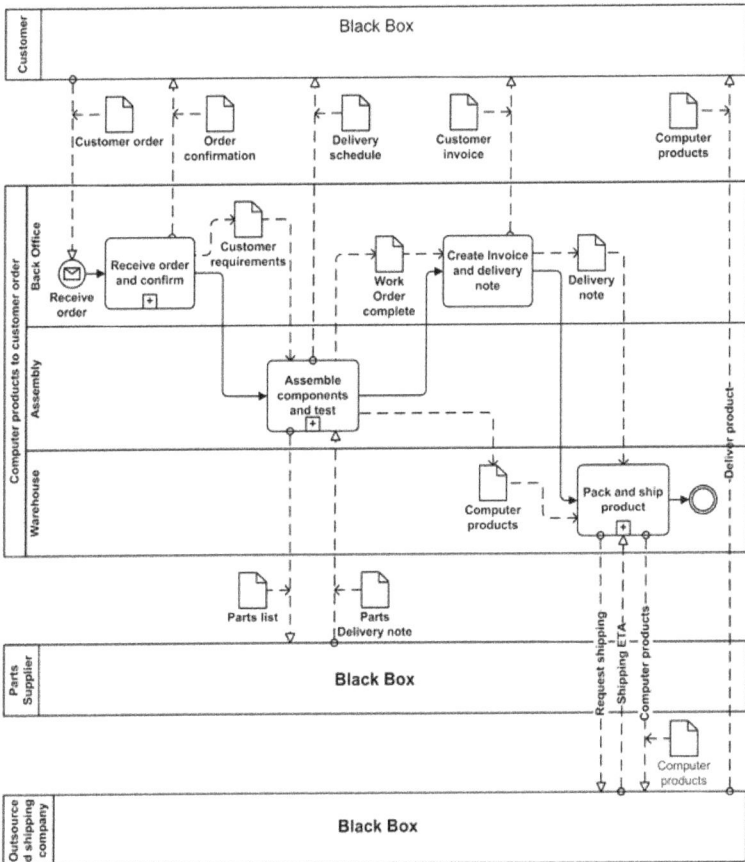

The business process sequence description

The **computer products to customer order** process is a white box pool and is broken into three specific swimlanes. The swimlanes represent the departments used in this process.

- back office
- assembly
- warehouse

Three process pools are designated as black box pools.

- outsourced shipping company
- parts supplier
- customer

The communication between the black box pools and the white box pool is shown using message flows.

The **customer** sends one document, customer order, which starts the process. The **customer** receives four different documents from the **computer products to customer order** process.

- order confirmation
- delivery schedule
- customer invoice
- delivery note included in the product packaging

The **parts supplier** receives a **parts list,** if new parts are required, and responds with an estimated delivery time for the new parts. The estimated delivery time will enable the **computer products to customer order** process, to confirm the delivery schedule to the customer. The new parts will be supplied accompanied by a parts delivery note.

The outsourced shipping company is requested for an estimated time of arrival (ETA) which will influence the delivery time to the customer.

Summary

- The use of these documents cannot be over emphasized and therefore their accuracy is paramount
- The documents described are a guide to what a company can produce for its own purposes
- It must be remembered that although the departments are shown as part of the process sequence, this may not be their only work load and they could be involved in other processes

Using these documents a business analyst would be able to model each sub-process and detail the individual document requirements.

15 Modelling Business Sub-processes

The previous chapter documented the new business process description of the Hardware Supplier company, **computer products to customer order** process. The following BPD shows the series of sub-processes required for the business process **computer products to customer order**.

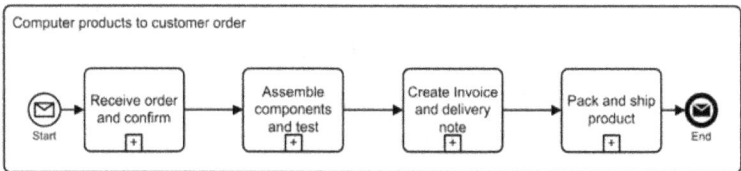

The following is a description of the four sub-processes required to complete the process.

Sub-processes

1. Receive order and confirm
2. Assemble components and test
   2.1 Test products
3. Create invoice and delivery note
4. Pack and ship product

Each one of these sub-processes is documented by a business process analyst and reviewed by the business process owner and fulfilment staff. The sub-processes are documented individually and each one described in detail on the following pages.

Sub-process 1 Receive Order And Confirm

Business process name

Computer products to customer order

Sub-process name

Receive order and confirm

Business process owner

To be designated

Business process analyst

To be designated

Tasks list

Receive and check for a valid order

Check customer database

Update customer database

Check credit

Check with finance to proceed

Create and send unable to complete order

Create and send confirmation of customer order

Create order requirements for assembly and payment

Description

The process receives an order from a new or existing customer and checks the customer database. If the customer is new, the database is updated. The customer credit status is checked with the finance department before proceeding. If the customer has a good credit rating an invoice will be sent on delivery of the products, otherwise the payment is COD. An order requirement is produced and passed to **assemble components and test.**

Trigger

Customer order

Results

Customer order requirements

Inputs

Customer order

Outputs

Customer requirements

Business rules

If the customer is not credit worthy, then the finance department will advise whether the order can be completed COD.

If the finance department advises against completing the order, notification is sent to the customer.

Interfaces

Customer

Notes

None

Receive Order And Confirm (BPD)

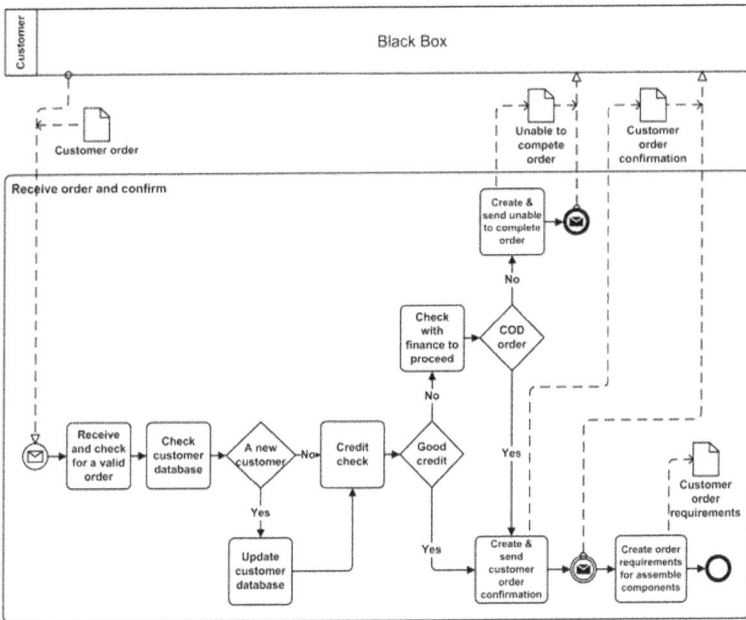

BPD description

- The order is received and the customer is checked on the database

- If customer credit is questionable, the finance department checks the credit rating before an order is processed.

- If the credit check is positive then the process continues with the order

- An order confirmation is sent to the customer and an order requirement is produced and sent to **assemble components and test**

- If the credit is questionable then the finance department advises whether to allow the order COD, otherwise the customer is informed the products cannot be delivered

Sub-process 2 Assemble Components And Test

Business process name

Computer products to customer order

Sub-process name

Assemble components and test

Business process owner

To be designated

Business process analyst

To be designated

Tasks list

Check requirements and create a work order

Check order against inventory

Create delivery schedule

Assemble products

Create a new parts list order

Receive new parts

Test product (sub-process)

Deliver products to packaging

Description

This sub-process accepts the order requirements, checks the parts availability, produces a work order and proceeds to assemble the product. After the product is tested it is moved to packaging and shipping

N.B: If parts are not available then the missing parts should be ordered. Testing could reveal bad components and therefore new components must be ordered.

Trigger

Customer order requirements

Results

Assembled and fully tested products to the customer requirements, delivered for packaging and shipping.

Inputs

Order requirements document

Outputs

Computer products

Work order (completed)

Customer delivery schedule

Business rules

The computer products will be assembled and tested within 10 working days.

Customer is sent a product delivery schedule within two working days of receiving the order requirements.

Customer is informed of any delays to the delivery schedule within one working day.

Interfaces

Customer

Parts supplier

Notes

The product testing is described as a separate sub-process **test products**.

Delivery delays procedure is not described in this document and will need further modelling.

Assemble Components And Test BPD

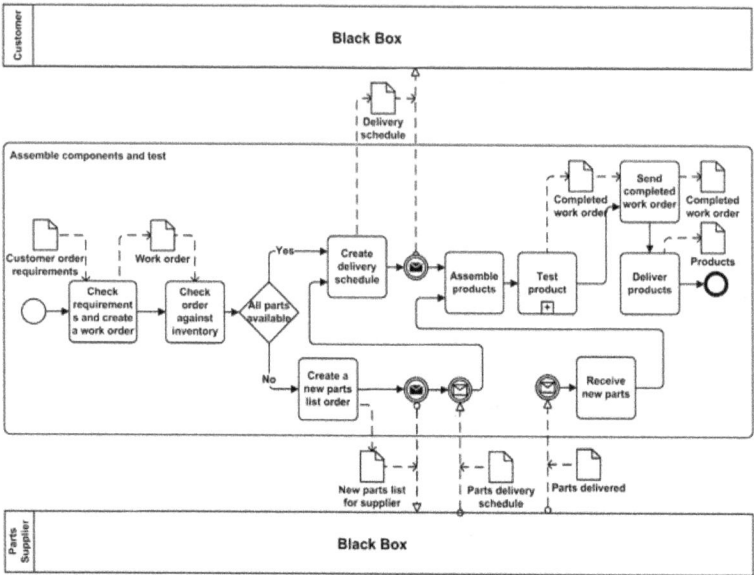

BPD description

- The customer order requirements are checked and a work order is produced

- If any parts are not in stock, then further parts are ordered from the parts supplier

- The customer is sent a delivery schedule

- The products are assembled and sent for testing

- When the work order is completed it is sent to **Create Invoice and delivery note**

- When the work order is completed the products are delivered to **Package product and ship goods**

Sub-process 2.1 Test Products

Business process name

Computer products to customer order

Sub-process name

Test product

Business process owner

To be designated

Business process analyst

To be designated

Tasks

Receive assembled product

Check assembled product against work order

Run basic hardware tests

Remedy hardware failures

Run basic software tests

Check system for errors and correct

Description

The computer products are tested for hardware and software errors.

Trigger

A computer product is delivered with a work order

Results

Fully tested computer products

Inputs

Customer product

Work order

Outputs

Tested customer products

Business rules

The computer products are tested within 2 working days.

Interfaces

None

Notes

This sub-process is part of the **Assemble components and test** sub-process.

Test Product BPD

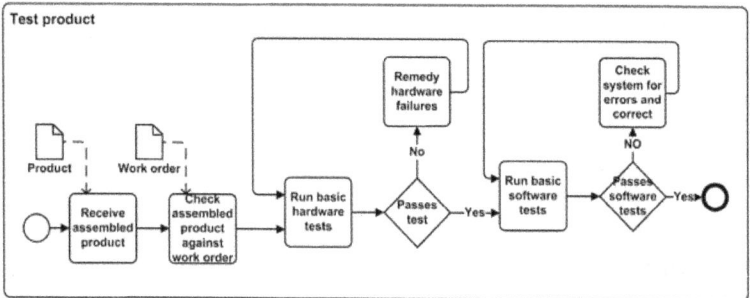

BPD description

- The products are received with a work order and are tested for hardware errors
- The products are tested with the ordered software

Sub-process 3 Create Invoice And Delivery Note

Business process name

Computer products to customer order

Sub-process name

Create invoice and delivery note

Business process owner

To be designated

Business process analyst

To be designated

Tasks list

Check work order against customer order

Create invoice

Create delivery note

Send invoice to customer

Forward invoice to warehouse

Forward delivery note to warehouse

Description

When the completed work order is received the customer invoice is produced along with the delivery note. If the customer is COD, then the invoice is provided with the delivery note to **package product and ship goods,** otherwise the invoice is sent directly to the customer.

Trigger

Completed work order

Results

Invoice is sent to the customer or if COD sent to **package product and ship goods.** The delivery note is sent to Package product and ship goods

Inputs

Work order compete

Outputs

Invoice

Delivery note

Business rules

An invoice will be produced and sent to the customer within one working day of receiving the completed work order.

In the case of COD both the invoice and the delivery note will be sent to **package product and ship goods**.

Interfaces

Customer

Notes

If the completed work order does not comply with the original customer order, then an escalation procedure is required.

Create Invoice And Delivery Note BPD

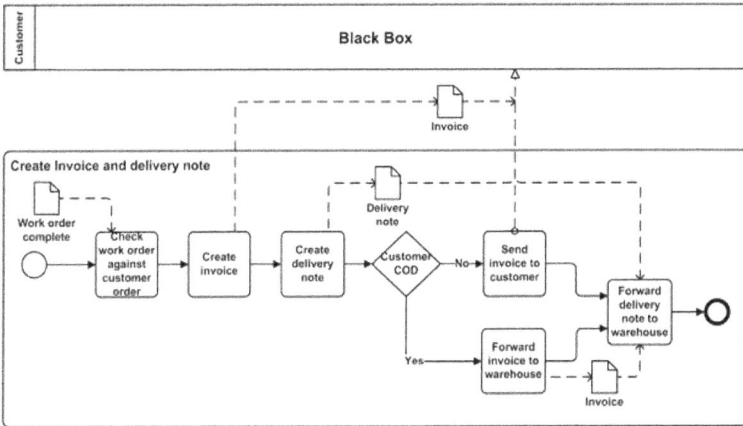

BPD description

- When a completed work order is received an invoice for the customer is produced along with a delivery note.

- If the customer has a good credit rating the invoice is sent directly to the customer, otherwise it is forwarded to **package product and ship goods**

- The delivery note is always sent to **Package product and ship goods**

Sub-process 4 Pack And Ship Product

Business process name

Computer products to customer order

Sub-process name

Pack and ship product

Business process owner

To be designated

Business process analyst

To be designated

Tasks

Receive product

Collect specific packaging material

Package product with delivery note

Find best shipping company for destination

Order shipping company

Create bill of lading

Place product in finished goods

Check finished goods

Handover all goods for shipment

Description

The product is package along with the delivery note. A shipping company is arranged and the goods handed over for delivery to the customer.

Trigger

Computer products with delivery note

Results

The computer products are packaged and handed over to a shipping company

Inputs

Computer product

Delivery note

Invoice in the case of COD

Outputs

Packaged computer products with delivery note

Invoice with COD

Business rules

A shipping company is selected that can deliver the products on time at the best price

Interfaces

Outsourced shipping company

Notes

The shipping company selection requires a procedure for selecting on time shipment, at the best price

Pack and ship product BPD

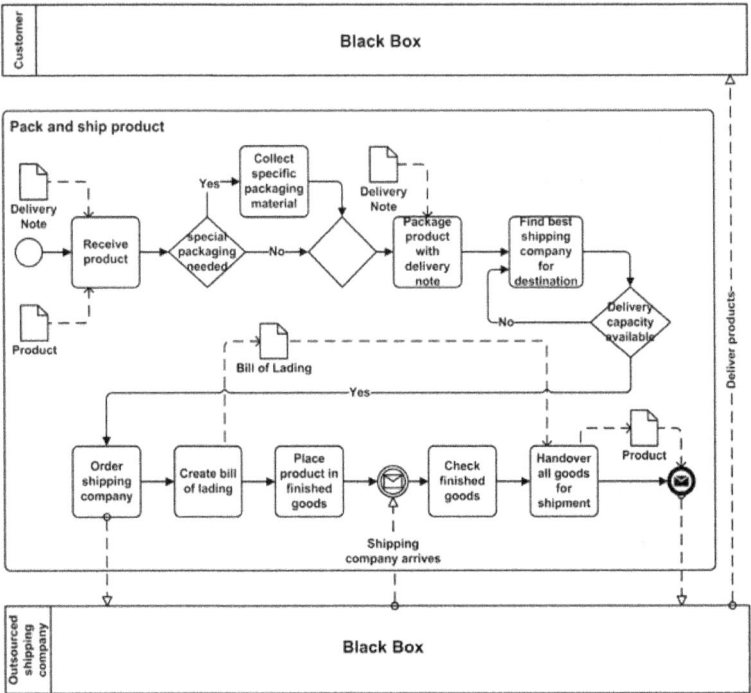

BPD description

- The received products are packaged with the delivery note

- The appropriate shipping company is selected, that will deliver on time, at the best price

- When the shipping company arrives, the goods are handed over with a Bill of Lading

16 Fulfilment Task Documents

This chapter describes the use of two types of documents provided to fulfilment staff for business process implementation.

1) Task procedure

2) Task method statement

Task Procedure

Tasks require a procedure to aid fulfilment staff to perform the tasks and produce outcomes. A procedure is a sequence of steps which the fulfilment staff should adhere to. This is called a **task procedure** document. This document can be used by business process fulfilment staff as a guideline on how to carry out the procedure.

Guidelines For A Task Procedure

Task name

The specific name describing the actual task

Process name

Associates the task with a specific process

Process ID/task no

Company business process identification and task number identification

Process analyst

The name of the analyst responsible for the work

Task description

> A detailed description of the **task procedure**, including the inputs and outcomes and describing the steps of the procedure

Procedure steps

> The sequential number of the procedure steps

Procedure step description

> Describes the steps in a manner understood by fulfilment staff

Task Procedure Example

In a previous chapter, the **Going to Work** process described a procedure for taking a shower. The following describes the basic requirements for a task procedure for taking a shower.

Task procedure for taking a shower	
Process name	Going to Work
Process ID/task no.	GTW/ta
Process analyst	Justin Little
Task Description	This procedure describes how a person will take a shower
Procedure steps	Procedure step description
1	Enter the bathroom
2	Turn on the taps both hot and cold
3	Wait and adjust to the correct temperature
4	Pull the shower curtain over

5	Start the shower
6	Remove pyjamas
7	Get in the shower
8	Find the shower soap
9	Lather up
10	Wash the soap off
11	Turn off shower taps
12	Pull the shower curtain back
13	Get out of the shower
14	Find the towel
15	Towel dry
16	Put on dressing gown
17	Leave the bathroom

Task Method Statement

A **task method statement** is a document used primarily for health and safety issues, detailing the way a business process task is to be completed and includes

- an outline of any hazards involved
- a step by step guide on how the task should be performed safely
- details of the control measures that are introduced to ensure the safety of anyone who is affected by the task

The business process manager should outline the requirements for each process task, in conjunction with the business owner. This should take into account the sequence of steps needed to complete a process task safely, with the minimum risk possible to the person carrying out the task.

Guidelines For A Task Method Statement.

Task name

The specific name describing the actual task

Process name

Associates the task with a specific process

Process ID/task no.

Company business process identification and task number

Process analyst

Name and position of the analyst responsible for the work

Task description

A description of the task, including the inputs and outcomes

Task details

The procedural sequence of events describing the safety factors and the risks where problems might occur

Competencies

Describes the competencies required by the fulfilment staff carrying out the task

Risks and potential hazards

This identifies the risks and potential hazards during the task sequence. Steps taken to reduce the risks are then determined

Health and safety

This includes all health and safety aspects of the task

Personal protection equipment

Outlines the protection equipment required by the fulfilment staff

Control of activity risks

Outlines any controls which are needed to reduce the risks while performing the task

Resources

A list of resources required to complete the task.

Procedure steps

The series of steps that are to be adhered to by the individual carrying out the task

Alternate or exception paths

Outlines any steps that might be taken as an alternative to the normal procedure or in the case of an exception to the procedure

Task Method Statement Example

In a previous chapter the **Going to Work** process described a procedure for taking a shower. The following describes the basic requirements for a **task method statement** for taking a shower.

Task method statement for taking a shower	
Process name	Going to Work
Process ID/task no.	*GTW/tam*
Process analyst	Justin Little
Task description	A person takes a shower
Task details	The person enters the bathroom, turns on the hot and cold taps. When the water is the right temperature the person steps into the shower. After washing hair and body the water is turned off and the person steps out of the shower and dries themselves with a towel.
Competencies	To be able to take a shower unaided
Risks and potential hazards	<ul><li>Burns from water being too hot</li><li>Electrical shock from a power source</li><li>The shower basin becomes slippery</li><li>The floor outside the shower becomes wet and slippery</li></ul>

	• Falling down while in the shower • Shower has a high step
Health and safety	The hot water must not be too hot and the bath or shower should not be slippery
Personal protection equipment	A shower hat
Control of activity risks	The bathroom is checked that no power connections are within reach of a person taking a shower. The towels and toilet articles are within reach of the shower. A mat is provided outside the shower in case the floor becomes wet. A handle is provided to hold while in the shower. A sign is provided to show the height of the shower basin before stepping in.
Resources	A towel, soap, shampoo, body lotion, a back scrubber
Procedure steps	The person taking the shower first checks that the shower basin is not slippery or a mat is provided. The water is turned on and checked that it is at the correct temperature before entering. After the shower is finished the person treads on a dry mat outside the shower.
Alternate or exception paths	If the shower basin is slippery and a mat is not provided, then the person taking a shower places a towel on the shower floor before stepping into the shower.

Summary

- A **task procedure** is a series of steps which are written down and followed by the person or persons carrying out the task

- The **task method statement** is a working level document that provides a description of the work to be undertaken, and should highlight any significant hazards, as well as hazards that could result from an associated task

- A **task method statement** is a sequence of steps to be adhered to, in order to reduce any risks including all health and safety aspects such as personal protective equipment requirements etc.

NOTES:

17 Role Of The Business Process Analyst

Much of the work of analysing and documenting business processes would be carried out by a business process analyst. The business process analyst is part of the business management team, interfacing to the different process operations.

Business Process Analyst

The role of a business process analyst is to concentrate on the requirements of improving existing or developing new business processes. The role includes

- Analysing existing processes and document if appropriate
- Documenting new and existing business rules
- Reviewing requirements with the stakeholders and developing the process model, including process steps, within constrains of the business rules
- Developing process procedures and training documentation
- Providing IT task documentation if process automation is required

Key Competences

- Works constructively within a team and builds rapport with team participants
- Gathers and presents business and process requirements
- Establishes facts
- Analyses impact of decisions

- Analyses trends and makes improvement recommendations

- Manages expectations

- Trains fulfilment staff

- Motivates task fulfilment staff to provide process requirements

- Understands strategy at process level

- General knowledge of industry

- Builds rapport with stakeholders

- Key report writing skills

- Business process mapping skills

Working Approaches

- Understand the statement of business requirements

- Understand and document the overall process

- Check the overall processes with the process manager, process owner and stakeholders

- Listen to the fulfilment staff and document their specific tasks for new and existing implementations

- Review the task documentation with selected fulfilment staff

- Present the process documentation to the process manager and process owner

- Train the fulfilment staff on the process tasks including the business rules

- Determine and document the process automation requirements

- Check process automation against the existing selected software

- Document use cases

- Encourage staff involvement by emphasising the positive changes which may include:
  - Improved working conditions
  - Clearly explained operating procedures alongside flexibility of working routines
  - Improved quality of product or service being provided
  - Participation in decision making
  - Effective training in new processes and procedures
- Business Process Analyst Skills
- Able to communicate and Interface at all levels from the task fulfilment staff to the upper management and stakeholders

- Able to analyse the required tasks and document them in a form that is easily understood

- Able to motivate staff to share their specific task information

- Negotiate the process requirements until an agreement is reached

- Write clear and precise documentation

- Determine which tasks need automation

- Document requirements to IT where process automation is required

- Able to adapt to different industries and their subsequent requirements

- Stay patient with staff who do not understand the role of the business process analyst

- Be sensitive when working with different cultures, ethnic groups and nationalities

Summary

- The business process analyst's prime objective is to analyse processes for companies

- Once requirements are approved, the analyst embarks on full documentation

- It is good practice for the business process analyst to review the documentation with the business owner and stakeholders

- After a process implementation, the analyst monitors the processes and calls regular review meetings to clarify any changes

- Many staff view process change in a negative manner, and yet through the business process analyst it is possible to achieve motivation along-side productivity improvement

- There is no end to business process improvement, it is an ongoing process

18   Revisiting Business Process Management

In today's world the customer dictates business requirements. Companies must look at the business processes they provide through the eyes of their customers. This may mean that companies should consider re-inventing themselves in order to become process centric, with business processes at the centre of their business.

To create and maintain a process centric business it is advantageous to use Business Process Management (BPM). BPM enables a company to successfully align business practices with strategic objectives and increase business performance.

Process Outside In - Not - Inside Out

The starting point in any company that wishes to become process centric is to look at how their customers or potential customers view them. This entails looking from the outside of the company into the company processes. In doing this, the following questions should be considered.

- Is the customer regarded as king

- Are the business processes regarded from a customer perspective (process from outside in)

- Is the company meeting customer expectations

- Are the customer expectations understood

- Are the company business processes fully tested as the customer would use them

- Do the customers accept inadequate services

Client Facing Processes

Moments of Truth

The **moments of truth** can be classified as, any time a customer uses a company's services. These moments are sometimes good and sometimes inadequate. Customers have become used to processes which do not reach expectations and give additional problems, which customers should not experience. The company should try to capture all customer problem areas and document them to be forwarded to process management on a regular basis.

The ultimate aim of the company should be to provide a good customer service that is superior to the competition.

Moments of truth

There are many **moments of truth** and often it is the front line personnel who have to contend with the failures of the company processes. The following are examples of moments of truth.

1. Buying a ticket for a train
2. Retrieving money from an ATM
3. Check out in a supermarket

There is an endless list of interactions with services which people are faced with every day. Some moments of truth are satisfactory and others are definitely inadequate.

Break Points

Behind each **moment of truth** lies a series of possible untold difficulties. These are called **break points.**

Examples Of Moments Of Truth

1) Buying a ticket for a train

Good moment of truth

If the ticket machine is working and prints a ticket and gives you the correct change, then you have received the service you were expecting.

Bad moment of truth

If the ticket machine is out of order, or does not print your ticket or you did not receive your correct change or no change was given, then the business process has broken down.

2) Retrieving money from an ATM

Good moment of truth

When withdrawing from a cash machine you receive the money you were expecting with a receipt, then the business process worked correctly.

Bad moment of truth

If the cash machine is out of order or does not accept your card or does not give out money or the wrong amount, then the business process has broken down.

3) Check out in a supermarket

Good moment of truth

If purchased goods go through the check out without packages breaking, with the correct amount as shown on the package and the correct change is given, then the process worked correctly.

Bad moment of truth

If a package bursts or the top comes off, or the sticker on the package is incorrect or incorrect change is given and the list of products purchased on the receipt does not correspond to the products in the basket, then the business process has broken down.

There are many instances where business processes produce the expected outcome and there also instances where processes break down. Customer feedback is vital and should not be underestimated when analyzing business process outcomes.

NOTES:

Capturing Client Facing Process Inadequacies

The following diagram describes the process for capturing customer feedback and producing process changes where necessary.

Capturing client facing process inadequacies

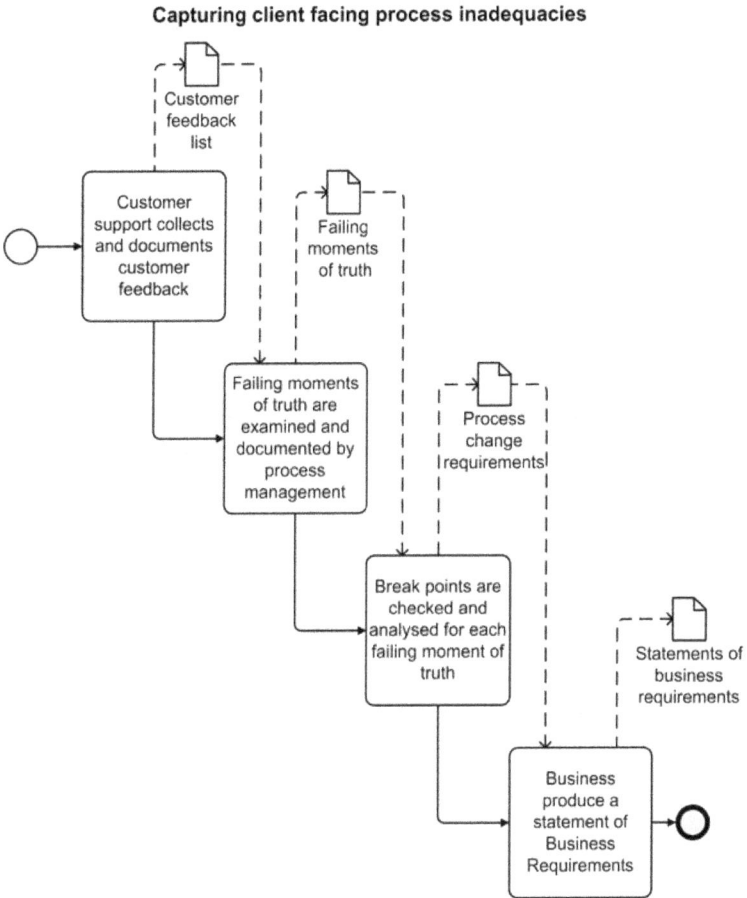

Description Of Client Facing Process Inadequacies

Customer support

Customer support must be vigilant and document all process inadequacies which appear while the process is in operation. The list of process inadequacies should be reviewed on a regular basis to establish changes and forwarded to process management.

Process management

The customer feedback list is examined and analysed for any necessary changes to the process. A list of failing moments of truth and their causes are documented.

Analysis of the individual process inadequacies are listed with the specific possible break points. The break points are identified and documented for process change requirements.

Business

The new business requirements are established from the process change requirements and a statement of business requirements is produced.

The Way Forward

In a process centric organisation the processes are reviewed to ascertain whether the needs of the customer are fulfilled. Examples of failing customer service should be documented and acted on.

Review how the customer sees the service, and what their expectations are.

Produce processes that fit the needs of the customer.

Always view the business process from the outside looking in and from the point of view of the customer.

Once a business process has been developed and deployed, manage the process as the customer environment changes. This requires constant process review and adjustment, to meet the changing business environment.

All business processes can be improved without necessarily introducing new technology.

A business process is not just about technology but strategy and people.

It is the technology that must fit the business process, not the business process adjusted to fit the technology.

Business Process Management (BPM) is a discipline that treats any business as a set of processes (business model).

Processes are company assets which are designed, controlled and managed within the organisation.

BPM is an End-To-End process and controls everything within the business.

External business focus is one of the main points in BPM and therefore needs to be supported at the most senior levels of management.

If true BPM is your goal, then you must consider all functions including incremental process improvements.

The meaning of **customer** can vary but it refers to the person or organisation receiving the service and is directly affected by that service.

The business process is driven by the company strategy and the business model.

The business process revolves around people fulfilling the tasks using technology, where and when required

NOTES:

Appendix

Business Process Documents

The following documents are described in this appendix

1. Statement of Business Requirements
2. Business Process Description
3. Sub-process Description
4. Task Method Statement
5. Task Procedure.

Statement Of Business Requirements

Company

Company name

Business process name

The name of the process (Verb - Noun)

Business process owner

The name and position of the process owner

Business process manager

The name and position of the process manager

Business process overview

This is a narrative view of the overall requirements of a new or improved process

Business process method

This describes how the process is performed

Resources

This describes the resources associated with the delivery of the process, largely drawn from the service requirements of other processes, internal or external.

Business rules

The required business rules are described and documented

Regulations

Regulations that influence the process are described and documented, such as internal and external company or organisation standards

Dependencies

Process dependences are described which influence the process activities and the use of appropriate standard tools.

Implementation plans

The process owner's plans for use and implementation is described

Business Process Description

Business process name

The name of the process (Verb - Noun)

Process ID

Company business process identification

Business process owner

The name and position of the process owner

Process manager

The name and position of the process manager

Business process analyst

The name of the process manager or analyst

Sub-processes

List of the sub-processes

Process description

A brief description of the business process in simple terms that can be understood by all personnel involved in the process

Process trigger

A description of the event, or events, which initiate or start the process

Process results

This describes the expected outcome and results of the process to be delivered

Process inputs

Process input requirements are defined in general terms and are listed

Process outputs

Process output requirements are defined in general terms and are listed

Process business rules

A list of the required business rules as specified by the statement of business requirements

Process interfaces

The process interfaces with other entities

Process notes

Notes about this process or other related processes

Business process overview

This is a high level business process diagram outlining the sub-process and the sequence flow

Business process document flow

This describes the documents that are to be produced for the customer and internal documents which are required for the process

Company process sequence

This describes the process sequence flow and where and when documents are an input and where documents are produced

Sub-process Description

Business process name

The name of the process (Verb - Noun)

Sub-process name

The name of the sub-process (Verb - Noun)

Process ID

Company business process identification

Business process owner

The name and position of the process owner

Process manager

The name and position of the process manager

Business process analyst

The name of the process manager or analyst

Sub-processes tasks list

The list of tasks to be carried out by the fulfilment staff as part of this sub-process

Sub-process description

The description of the sub-process

Sub-process trigger

The sub-process trigger(s)

Sub-process results

The results of the sub-process

Sub-process inputs

The input requirements i.e. documents

Sub-process outputs

The output requirements i.e. documents

Sub-process business rules

The business rules designated for this sub-process

Sub-process interfaces

Specific interfaces with other entities

Sub-process notes

Notes about this sub-process or other related processes

Sub-process BPD

The BPD of the sub-process

The description of the sub-process BPD

Task Method Statement

Task name

The specific name describing the actual task

Process name

Associates the task with a specific process

Process ID/tasks no.

Company business process identification and task number

Process analyst

Name and position of the analyst responsible for the work

Task description

A description of the task, including the inputs and outcomes

Task details

The procedural sequence of events describing the safety factors and the risks where a problem might occur

Competencies

Describes the competencies required by the fulfilment staff carrying out the task

Risks and potential hazards

This identifies the risks and potential hazards during the task sequence. Steps taken to reduce the risks are then determined

Health and safety

This includes all health and safety aspects of the task

Personal protection equipment

Outlines the protection equipment required by the fulfilment staff

Control of activity risks

Outlines any controls which are needed to reduce the risks while performing the task

Resources

A list of resources required to complete the task

Procedure steps

The series of steps that are to be adhered to, by the individual carrying out the task

Alternate or exception paths

Outlines any steps that might be taken as an alternative to the normal procedure or in the case of an exception to the procedure

Task Procedure

Task name

The specific name describing the actual task

Process name

Associates the task with a specific process

Process ID/task no

Company business process identification and task number identification

Process analyst

The name of the analyst responsible for the work

Task description

A detailed description of the task procedure, including the inputs and outcomes and describing the steps of the procedure

Procedure steps

The sequential number of the procedure step

Procedure step

Describes the step event so that it can be understood by the fulfilment staff

Procedure steps	Procedure step description
1	Step 1 description
2	Step 2 description
3	Step 3 description
4	Step 4 description

Kenneth J Sherry

Hopes this book has given you an insight into business processes and invites your comments and feedback.

www.admaks.com

Kenneth@admaks.com